Anthony Bailey—called by *The New York Times* "a perceptive observer and reporter" and by *The New Yorker* "a gifted writer who . . . can make everything around him come alive"—is also the author of two novels and three nonfiction books. His most recent book was the much-loved *The Thousand Dollar Yacht,* and he has written of the environments men create for themselves in *Through the Great City* and *The Inside Passage.* Mr. Bailey's work has also appeared in *The New York Times, Horizon,* and *The New Yorker,* for which he is a staff writer.

Mr. Bailey was born in England in 1933 and educated at Oxford. He now lives in Stonington, Connecticut, with his wife and four daughters.

The
Light
in
Holland

Alfred A. Knopf
New York
1970

The Light in Holland

🌷

ANTHONY BAILEY

THIS IS A BORZOI BOOK
PUBLISHED BY ALFRED A. KNOPF, INC.

Library of Congress Catalog Card Number: 78-118705

Most of the material in this book appeared in
The New Yorker in slightly different form.

Manufactured in the United States of America

FIRST EDITION

Very much for Margot

Other Voices

Eugène Fromentin: "Whoever speaks of a northern corner of the earth with water, woods, maritime horizons, speaks by that very fact of a universe in small. In its relation to the tastes and instincts of those who observe carefully, the smallest country, scrupulously studied, becomes an everlasting field of discovery, as crowded as life, as fertile in sensations as the heart of man is fertile in ways of feeling."

John Lothrop Motley: "It is impossible for a nation, while struggling for itself, not to acquire something for all mankind."

Hippolyte Taine: "It is impossible in such a country to imagine philosophers such as we find in Germany, or excursions into the realm of fantasy or systems of metaphysics. One is quickly brought to earth: the desire for action is too universal, too urgent and too incessant: thought is only taken with a view to action."

Baruch Spinoza: "The more perfection anything has, the more active and the less passive it is: and contrariwise, the more active it is, the more perfect it becomes."

Other Voices

George Canning: "The fault of the Dutch is giving too little and asking too much."

J. C. van Schagen: "There are too many of us. We have no space, either materially or spiritually. We don't rob trains. We never blow anything up."

Jan van Ruysbroeck: "God in the depths of us receives God who comes to us: it is God contemplating God."

First De Stijl Manifesto, 1917: "There is an old and a new consciousness of time. The old is based on the individual; the new is based on the universal."

Leonard Woolf: "Whenever I go to Holland, I feel at once that I have reached the apotheosis of bourgeois society. The food, the comfort, the cleanliness, the kindliness, the sense of age and stability, the curious mixture of beauty and bad taste, the orderliness of everything including even nature and the sea—all this makes one realize that here on the shore of the dyke-controlled Zuider Zee one has found the highest manifestation of the complacent civilization of the middle classes."

The Duke of Alva: "Holland is as near to hell as possible."

Johan Huizinga: "Devotion and a sense of duty are all we can undertake to bring to our deeds."

Sir William Temple: "Strangers among them are apt to complain of the spleen."

Contents

PART ONE: The Country as a Crowd

1

PART TWO: The Country as a Park

61

PART THREE: The Country as a Community

167

Index
follows page 263

PART ONE

❦

The
Country
as a
Crowd

"Your floor is my ceiling."

❦

❧ 1 ❧

PEOPLE USED TO GO TO HOLLAND because of art and costume, windmills and wooden shoes. I went because it is the most densely populated country in the world. In the United States roughly fifty-two people live on an average square mile; in Holland, nine hundred and seventy. Put another way, if the United States were as thickly settled as the Netherlands, it would be inhabited by over three billion people, which is more than the present total population of the world. "Holland," strictly speaking, is the name of the two provinces of north and south Holland, but common usage reinforced by the dominant role of those provinces has made it the popular name for the whole country, and I have used it and the Netherlands interchangeably to describe this scrap of space, which—it seemed to me—might be informative about the relationship between a great and growing number of human beings and their environment. I was interested in how people live in a small amount of land often obtained and held at high cost. I wanted to know some of the answers they might have found for how to make use of land, air, and water, and even how to live long, sanely, and prosperously. The nineteenth-century German poet Heine is alleged to have said, "If the world comes to an end I shall go to Holland—there everything happens fifty years later." I thought that today Heine's remark might be reversed—that it might be possible to see in Holland some aspects of the world fifty years from now; and, for that matter, if the world were coming to an end, perhaps with a brainstorm rather than with a bang, the first signs of it might appear in Holland, giving us some warning.

❧ 2 ❧

"LITTLE" IS A TERM MUCH USED IN HOLLAND. It comes not so much as a separate word, *klein,* but as the suffix *-je,* attached to the end of almost any word, like *straatje,* little street, or *huisje,* little house. A *dubbeltje* is a small coin worth ten Dutch cents and *meisje* is a young miss; if she is a very little girl she might be called a *klein meisje.* The diminutive bespeaks deprecation (*kippetjes* are not only little chickens but ladies of little virtue) and affection (*poffertjes* are scrumptious minature pancakes). "Come on, Pietje," one says to one's friend Piet, who is pie-eyed drunk and needs to be helped homeward lest he fall and knock his head against the *kinderhoofdjes,* tiny heads of little children, the nickname for the cobblestones still used together with bricks for hand-paving the streets and sidewalks of this always sinking and settling land. The

Dutch like small things. They cherish objects, knick-knacks, mementoes, like dried flowers, seashells, pieces of wood or porcelain, all talismans and touchstones. In Scheveningen one day I met a hydraulic engineer who had on his desk three small bricks he couldn't refrain from caressing; they were from a house that was being built for him, one red-brown, one grey, and one glazed black, each brick not only with its own color and texture but its own response to the light and climate of the moment. The Dutch often insist that big things are not for them; for example, Rotterdam and The Hague have never been properly incorporated as cities; they are villages; and if Amsterdam is a city, at least it is a relatively small and cosy city. What is small has value. One can cope with it, look after it, find its proper place, and properly maintain it. It was a Dutchman, Anton van Leeuwenhoek (1632–1723) who perfected the microscope; he was the first man to see a microbe.

Holland is a little country—thirteen thousand nine hundred and sixty-seven square miles, or about the size of Massachusetts and Connecticut lumped together—and you can drive from one end of it to the other in the time it takes to get from New York to Providence, or London to Sheffield. Almost every public telephone booth contains the telephone directories for the entire country. In this small space some parts have less room than others; in the west of Holland, where a number of cities and towns are connected in a horseshoe-shaped ring the Dutch call the Randstad, or Ring-City, the population is four times more dense than it is in the country as a whole. But

the Dutch have a great deal of experience in tight fit and
the thrifty use of space. Stairs rise in Alpine gradients; on
some ascents you bump your knees against the treads as
you climb. Escalators in department stores are similarly
steep, and the elevator in the office building of the Rotterdam Planning Department has room for three planners before lunch in one of the prosperous Lijnbaan restaurants,
and two afterward. Two and sometimes three people are to
be seen riding on one bicycle. In Amsterdam cemeteries,
unless you've paid an extra fee for long-term tenure, you
lose your occupation rights after twenty years. (Several
new crematoria are presently being built.) There is
civilian pressure on military authorities to use what are
called shooting cinemas instead of full-scale, space-
consuming rifle and artillery ranges. Bathtubs are rare.
Although all new houses and flats have showers, the
right of people to sit and brood while soaking has not
been recognized in Holland. In their one-and-a-half-room
flat in Amsterdam, a young couple I know, called the
Heermas, have a bed which folds out of a sort of side-
board behind the dining table; but then the Dutch have
been going to bed in cupboards for centuries, and often
the children slept in a drawer underneath their parents.
Even today they don't seem to mind bumping into one
another. They push and jostle as if they were in a constant football crowd or subway train, not shrinking from
physical contact with strangers the way North Americans
do. When you have found room to sit in a crowded train
your next occupation is finding space on the floor to place
your feet in the room left by other feet. Ordinary week-

day shopping conditions in most of the Randstad towns resembles that inside a New York department store at Christmas: it is elbow to elbow, and sometimes elbow to rib. The sidewalks were never wide. The insouciant stranger steps casually off the curb to let two plump matrons pass and hears a yell as a bicycle rider bumps into him and then ricochets off the side of a fortunately very slowly moving tram. I paused one day in Leiden, crossing an unfamiliar street, and looked down at my map. Poor tourist! There had been no traffic in sight, but suddenly a small Simca hurtled round the corner and screeched to a slow-down a few yards from me. Then, since I stood there stupefied, it threateningly jerked forward and halted again, like a gun to my stomach, one bumper an inch from my kneecaps. My unconsidered reaction at being thus menaced was to shake my fist at the driver. The Dutch are supposed to be stolid, untemperamental types, but this man at once got out of his car and began to shout at me. I, in return, in furious English, suggested he jump in the nearest canal, which was about ten feet behind him. He now saw his Dutch oaths were of no avail and, shaking with thwarted aggression, screamed, "Stupid American!" and then, for good measure, "God damned Englishman!" Then he got back in his car and blasted away. At the time, which was early in my Randstad days, I thought him a psychopath, but I came to understand him.

A small land containing a lot of people: the Dutch are constrained by this. They don't indulge in sweeping gestures or extravagant hospitality. The only big gestures in Holland are "The Night Watch," by Rembrandt, and the Baroque organ in St. Bavo's Church in Haarlem, both more than two hundred and fifty years old. As for hospitality, things haven't changed much since David Dalrymple wrote in 1763 to James Boswell, who was studying in Utrecht, "It may well be that you have found Dutch civility a little dry. . . . The Dutch do not give dinners, they do not put themselves at the trouble of paying visits."

The concern for little things runs alongside the idea that everything has its value or price, which in turn now and then gives rise to a compulsive pennypinching and moneygrubbing. A Dutch landlord, seeing a small chip of paint missing from the front door of an apartment he has rented you for two months, will probably think of charging you for repainting the whole flat, will try to charge you for repainting the complete door, and will certainly insist on working out a price for the chip or nick. What compensates for this is the sense of care and detail. In the apartment I came to know quite well, the living room was roughly what you see when you glance in while walking past the picture window of any Dutch house—a "picture" which brings to mind Leonard Woolf's phrase, "a curious mixture of beauty and bad taste." Many of the objects, big and small, are in bad taste; but the whole thing, the still life, is brilliantly arranged, is in a way beautiful. A sliding glass partition may divide a long room into two smaller rooms. There are two fireplaces, with thermostatically controlled gas heaters, warming the drawing-room area and the dining area. On the dining table and side tables carpets are spread. Embroidered mats cover the tops of the grandfather clock and the large radio (which has long-, medium-, and several short-wave bands bringing in stations from all over Europe), perhaps because it is easier to shake a mat out of a window than dust these surfaces. In the bookcase, together with works by Vondel, Couperus, and Pearl Buck, are books on the reclamation of the Zuider Zee (a scheme which is the pride and interest of every Dutchman) and on Australia, to which he may at one time have thought of emigrating. Standing and hanging are lamps of considerable ghastliness. On the walls hang several heavily framed paintings of calm cows or angry seas and a few drawings, nicely drawn—a girl's head, a flower. Everywhere, of course, there are flowers and plants, on the broad, tile-surfaced windowsill, on the mantelpiece, in wall racks and holders—a vase of early tulips, and potted cactus, azaleas, geraniums, rubber plants. The floor is linoleum-tiled or parquet. There are velvet cushions and a good carpet; the sofa also has a rug over it to save wear and tear. The large bulky cabinet, which may be antique or reproduction, has room for family valuables like linen, silver, documents, and souvenirs. And all around, standing on the molding over the partition's sliding doors, suspended in brackets above the fireplace and radio or on little shelves and corners that seem to exist for no other purpose, are all manner of small objects: small brass or copper things, powder horns, candle snuffers, antique oil lamps, paperweights, stuffed birds, embroidered samplers, seashells, a jar of colored sand, a sheet of exotic postage stamps, a photograph of a

Sumatran hillside, some peacock feathers, a straw basket, a piece of coral, a pistol, an ivory fan. When Rembrandt went bankrupt in 1656 an inventory was taken of his possessions. It took twenty pages to list the collection of objects which decorated his walls and filled his cupboards; he was, in this as in so many other things, a Dutchman. The Dutch are the great materialists; they love *things*.

Things are not just small in Holland; mostly, they are in scale. Of course, in Holland as in other rapidly urbanizing countries life is subject to what planners call "scale-enlargement"—one lives in a fragment of a large development rather than in a separate small house; instead of traveling with other people in a slow canalboat, one can travel independently by car across the country in a few hours. However, the design of most new Dutch developments attempts to preserve or create those features—such as water, grass, trees, playgrounds, places to walk or sit and talk—which enhance one's feeling of being human and human-size. For that matter, if one throws a leg over the saddle of one of the seven million Dutch bicycles and starts pedaling, Holland no longer seems such a small country. I lived for a while with my family in Katwijk, which used to be a small fishing village in the coastal dunes between Scheveningen and IJmuiden, and is now a busy seaside resort and dormitory town for Leiden. Katwijk's traffic is fierce, but it is a good mixture: not just big trucks and big cars with one person in them, but big trucks, tiny trucks, bicycles, motor-assisted bicycles (which are called *bromfietsen,* or *brommers*), cars, buses, delivery wagons (hand-, pedal-, or motor-propelled), horse-wagons, and pushcarts. In the narrow Voorstraat, one-way for cars and trucks and perilously two-way for bikes and *brommers*, a chicken often hovers on the edge of the sidewalk, occasionally stepping forward to peck at a grain lying in a crack between two road bricks, looking as if he is about to cross, and causing bikes to swerve and cars to honk. Across the road is the local branch of Albert Heijn's chain of supermarkets. It is a spacious, ultra-modern store, with the supermarket virtue of lots of goods at low prices, and yet still something of the atmosphere of a family grocery store. There is, for instance, a notice board on which local people can post free advertisements: baby carriage for sale, racing pigeon wanted, Citroen 2cv *in goede staat* going cheap. Once a week I noticed a fishing trawler, captained by a Katwijk man, going by on the way to IJmuiden up the coast. It always swung in close to the Katwijk beach and blew several blasts on the horn. At this, children playing in the sand jumped up and down, and people waved; it pleased all the old men who remembered the days thirty years or so ago when wooden fishing boats were hauled up daily on the strand by horses, and a man could walk home from his vessel in five minutes. This Katwijk skipper still made a point of keeping in touch. I liked to think that, hearing those long blasts, one of the children ran into the town to the skipper's house, and told his wife that the trawler was on its way to IJmuiden, and the great man would be home to dinner.

In one place, however, Holland seems smaller than it is. Madurodam is a collection of miniature buildings, representative of old and new Holland, together with miniature docks, airport, churches, castles, factories, forests, bulb fields, windmills, television towers, apartment blocks, farms, an "aquatic sports center," marshaling yards, cheese manufactories, lifeboat stations, and so forth. It was begun as a memorial to a young Dutch soldier, George Maduro, who died at Dachau, and profits go to the Dutch Student Sanatorium. Situated near The Hague, Madurodam may be to Holland what Disneyland is to the United States or Madam Tussaud's is to England, largely a tourist attraction, but it demonstrates better than anything else the Dutch obsession with the diminutive. The scale is 1 to 25. Nearly fifteen million people have visited Madurodam, and I imagine that many of them, particularly the Dutch, have felt like Gulliver as they walked along its two miles of winding paths in an open amphitheater the size of a large skating rink, peering down at models of the Oranjeboom brewery, a typical Hague traffic jam ("caused by bicycles," says a label), and the new American Express offices, and chuckling as they bring the Amsterdam-Rotterdam bank into their Nikon viewfinder or slip a real life-sized *dubbeltje* into the mechanism that actuates the scaled-down barrel organ. In real life, on city streets, the organ grinder plays without prior payment, but he knows that at least one passerby out of twenty-five will hand out a coin.

An interesting time to visit Madurodam is on a Sunday afternoon in the bulb season, in spring. Find—if you can —a parking space, and then hold your own in the struggle to reach the ticket window with the horde of passengers just disembarked from six tour buses. Within, the advertised two miles of paths are seen to be wound as tightly as human intestines. The immediate effect is of a doll's house rock garden packed with giants (Dutch, Germans, Belgians, Americans, French, and English)—for the most part giant old ladies with large cameras—a child's size town with no room for children, in which children, in fact, are being lost, trodden upon, and pushed aside by adults out of Hieronymus Bosch. If you throw out an arm to rescue a whimpering child you find your elbow in a Teutonic bosom, your wrist in front of a Japanese Yashikaflex, and your shoulder being nudged by a Dutchman in the tight-packed line behind you as he leans aside to glimpse the miniature bulb field irrigated by water of just the right, murky, peat-colored shade. Except for half a dozen goldfish, looking like pink whales in a pond, the scale seems correct. Architectural details such as gables, tiles, towers, chimneys, and pigeon lofts would be interesting to a student or historian. But the whole thing is a bit like looking at the world through binoculars that have been dropped, in which one eyepiece magnifies and the other doesn't, and the effect is jumbled and headsplitting. You have a feeling like seasickness—and as that is apparently brought on by disturbed balance, so this sudden onrush of claustrophobia, hitting you in the head and stomach, may be induced by visual distortion—the world gone awry.

"*Achtung! Achtung!*" It is the loudspeakers, blaring a request that Fraulein Gesundheit report to Number 5 bus from Düsseldorf. You dream for a moment that the Dutch have taken their revenge—surely the Fraulein has been miniaturized into a one-twenty-fifth-size passenger of a model tourist bus caught in a Hague traffic jam on the way to a scaled-down version of Randstad Holland. Or is it possible that this apotheosis of the diminutive is a revenge the Dutch have taken upon themselves?

❦ 3 ❦

THE RANDSTAD is a horseshoe-shaped belt of towns, cities, and suburban settlement, with the base of the horseshoe on the North Sea dunes and its open end facing southeast. It is about thirty miles across, and if you straightened it out it would be roughly one hundred and ten miles long. It runs from Dordrecht through Rotterdam, Schiedam, Delft, The Hague, Leiden, Katwijk, Noordwijk, Sassenheim, Lisse, Zandvoort, Haarlem, IJmuiden, Zaandam, Amsterdam, Bussum, Hilversum, Amersfoort, to Utrecht. In what a Dutch architect I know calls, sardonically, the magical year 2000, some six billion people may live on earth and two thirds of them in cities —not only a population explosion but an urban explosion for which the Randstad may be a useful forerunner. In it at the moment live 4.34 million people, 37 per cent of the Dutch populace dwelling on 5 per cent of the Dutch land area.

Despite the fact that half the Randstad would be submerged if there were no dikes or dunes, water is what made it. The Dutch towns and cities became wealthy with marine trade in the seventeenth century, and although a slack period followed, their situation at the mouth of the Rhine has brought prosperity again. The catchment areas of the Rhine, the Meuse, and the Scheldt, which cover the old realm of Lothair (*ca.* 843), today hold the largest concentration of cities and industry in Europe. Within a radius of six hundred kilometers of the Rhine mouth live 200 million people—about 50 per cent of Europe's population. Its heart is the Ruhr, which after 1871 became Europe's greatest industrial area and caused the Rhine to become Europe's major commercial artery. The Rhine in turn promoted Holland and particularly the Randstad. There the economic functions of a metropolis have always been spread out rather than monopolized. Government has become the function of The Hague, sea commerce that of Rotterdam, finance and culture that of Amsterdam. Other towns had their own special trades and skills which brought them separate success. But in the nineteenth century the towns and cities of the Randstad began to acknowledge each other more directly through the growth of a fast, efficient railway system, and after 1900 suburbs spread along these lines of communication. Presently there are still small stretches of open space between most of them, and in the center of the horseshoe, what is unique in a conurbation of this size, a green heart or core.

There are other indispensable facts about the Randstad. Holland has the highest population growth rate in West-

ern Europe; its birth rate is the highest in Europe and its
death rate the lowest. For comparison, in the United
States deaths are 9.5 per thousand, births 18.5 per thousand, excess of births over deaths 9 per thousand. The
Dutch figures are, respectively, deaths, 8.1; births, 19.2;
excess of births over deaths, 11.1. For that matter, not
only are a lot of babies born in Holland; a lot of them
live. While the United States infant-mortality rate is
higher than that of seventeen other countries, that in
Holland is the lowest in the world. There, too, a child has
a better chance of living longer than he would elsewhere,
with an average life expectancy of 71.1 years for men
and 75.9 for women. Added to these natural factors is the
radiating power of the Randstad: people want to work
and live not in the wide, open spaces of Friesland,
Drenthe, or Overijssel, but in the small section of the
country which is already crowded to the extent of some
six thousand people per square mile. On any sunny Sunday you can see the principle demonstrated on the beach
which runs twenty-five miles from Scheveningen to
Zandvoort. Hundreds of thousands of people cluster together on the sands in front of the town boulevards, while
between these blobs of sun- and sea-bathing humanity
are long stretches of more or less desolate beach. We
gather in cities to assuage our loneliness.

Holland, in fact, is an excellent reminder that figures
and statistics about growth-rates and densities have always to be tempered with impressions and feelings—with
the likes and dislikes of people and what they are used to.
I wasn't long in Holland before I realized that one could
feel a great deal more "crowded," more hemmed-in in a

not particularly dense town the size of Katwijk, than one would in a teeming city like Amsterdam. Katwijk, for one thing, had far fewer distractions than Amsterdam: one was more conscious there of the apparatus of life. A small grubby apartment in Amsterdam might easily be considered a foothold for enjoying a marvelously various city. In Katwijk such an apartment would always be in the forefront of one's life. But even so, you shouldn't speak lightly about it. Anything with a roof and four walls is hard to come by, and you learn a lot about crowdedness in Holland when you attempt to find a place to live.

For the Dutch, their housing shortage has been with them so long it has ceased to have much news value. (They had a serious housing shortage in the seventeenth century.) Nowadays municipal authorities and housing associations (who build most houses and apartments) claim that there is no longer a serious quantitative housing shortage—the shortage is in terms of quality, and at that, quality in terms of space and construction standards rather than decay and dirt. There are few slums, but quite a lot of people live in improved garden sheds and made-over garages. In Katwijk during the summer season many couples are forced out of small flats and summer houses they are renting to make room for better-paying German tourists; at the end of August the Dutch tenants are let back in again. Where they have been staying in the meantime—at mother's, or in camping tents—is their own disconsolate concern. Mrs. Ham, a young woman in Katwijk, who came to help us keep our rented apartment in the spotless condition demanded by the land-

lord, was in that predicament, and she had been looking
for two years for somewhere to live in Wassenaar, five
miles away, where her husband worked. Because they are
unable to find more spacious accommodation, large families live in a pair of spotless rooms, and somehow don't go
mad. Bathrooms and kitchens are shared. Some couples
deliberately have children earlier than they want them in
order to get a better position on a waiting list. In some
areas houses are allocated to people with a job in the area
and the right number of children; a man buying a house
would have to meet these same specifications; a man selling his house would have to find a purchaser who met
them. Bribes and key-money are willingly paid if you can
find someone willing to give up an apartment for them.
Five thousand guilders, or about one thousand four hundred dollars, was the fee one couple I know paid to get a
two-bedroom flat outside of Amsterdam. Houseboats
would be fine, except houseboats cost about as much as a
house of comparable size and quality, and the places
where you can moor them conveniently are severely restricted and licensed. Many people live "illegally" in
various abodes, having claimed qualifications they didn't
have, or having promised not to rat on a landlord who
had been ordered by housing authorities to make improvements he didn't intend to make. Around the Dapperstraat in Amsterdam—an area the Amsterdam municipal authorities term a slum, but one which strikes anyone
who has walked through the back streets of any older
English or American city as merely, and cheerfully,
grubby—there are many nineteenth-century, five-story

tenement houses whose foundations are rotten. The houses are settling, the walls are cracking, and they will all be pulled down in the next ten years or so. The landlords are therefore reluctant to maintain them. Yet within, many residents are happy to have a home of their own at rents low even by Dutch standards. (The young Heermas pay ten dollars a month for their one-and-a-half rooms.) And within those deteriorating shells, many have made themselves comfortable with paneled walls and bright carpets. They aren't going to complain about dark stairs, sloping floors, and an unpainted front door.

The attempt being made to relieve the crowded housing situation is evident everywhere in the Randstad. The famous flat Dutch horizon, once interrupted only by church towers, barns, windmills, and clumps of trees, is now also broken by tall cranes leaning like giraffes over apartment buildings under construction. In the last decade roughly 40 per cent of all new Dutch building has been in the form of apartments, and in the west of Holland, where space is at a greater premium and the demand for accommodation is greater, the percentage has naturally been higher. A rapidly increasing population of smaller families, getting married earlier, not wanting to live with mother-in-law, and making a good living, has generated a huge need for living space. The general sogginess of Randstad soil and the huge expense of making it fit for building on are the basic reasons why a Dutchman cannot go out and build his own home on a plot of ground; he has to take what the community can manage to build for him. The Dutch in any event are not "possessive" in an English or American landowning sense. Perhaps because they realize the ever-sinking land is not theirs for eternity, property has no sacrosanct character for them. Even in conservative farming villages like Staphorst, the farmers have seen the benefit of land-reparceling schemes, with larger and economically more viable units being made and dispossessed farmers given priority for farms in the new polders of reclaimed land. Less than one third of Dutch dwellings are owner-occupied. Much land is owned by the state or by municipalities, and nowadays many Dutchmen find themselves tenants of municipalities or housing associations (backed in many cases by private industry), living in five- or six-story blocks, "system-built" with prefabricated parts designed by a Swede or made under an English license—for the international style of architecture has been followed by an international method of building. Some planning and housing departments of Dutch cities are a trifle defensive about their recent construction, but their apology is, "Well, you don't know the political pressure we've been under. We've just had to build a lot of accommodation cheaply and fast." A few Dutch architects say bluntly they have been building the slums of tomorrow.

If this is so, it isn't obvious at a glance. In fact, Randstad examples of big dormitory developments like Slotervaart and Osdorp, west of Amsterdam, or Pendrecht and the Prinz Alexander Polder outside Rotterdam, have immediately redeeming details and qualities. They have brightly colored balconies. They have places to stand bicycles and little ramps, alongside flights of steps, on which baby carriage or bike wheels can run. They have areas set aside for people to wash or tinker with their cars and—Prinz Alexander Polder being a conspicuous failure in this respect—generally many pools, ponds, basins, and canals where the necessity of having to drain and store water has been a gift to an otherwise drab landscape, the water forming another dimension, like a mirror enlarging an otherwise small room. Shops are often close at hand, the buildings form courtyards, and there is always a spot where many of the old people who have special flats in such developments can sit on benches by the canals and watch children play in sand-boxes. Some fish. Some simply watch the ducks glide.

And yet. The English planner Gerald Burke lived briefly in Slotervaart and came to think it was "too orderly, too inflexible, too complete, with few agreeable surprises and absolutely nothing left to chance. Preoccupied with the public welfare of a community, the designers appear to have overlooked the private welfare of a family." Osdorp, he decided, had "intimidating proportions." Dr. Arie Querido, an eminent Dutch physician who has been Public Health director of Amsterdam, an adviser in the planning of these new developments, and is now professor of Social Medicine at the University of Amsterdam, believes that construction standards have often been too low, so that people are disturbed by "noise, and other people's cooking, which never smells as good as one's own. Moreover, some of the design is bad. Some buildings are too tall—all you can see from them is the sky. Others lack privacy. Before the war all Dutch flats had their own ground-floor front door, and people living on the third and fourth floors climbed a dark and narrow staircase to reach their own homes. But they felt the flats were their own homes. There wasn't a common balcony running along in front of them."

To a foreigner this lack of privacy seems immensely real, though the Dutch now and then give one cause to wonder if it is so to them. They seem to be compelled to show they don't need to be private. They have always liked big windows. Row houses, in long terraces, depend on windows in front and back walls for all their light. In the seventeenth century the tall mullioned windows with the lower half shuttered let in that light, softly reflected off a white or yellow interior wall, you see in the paintings by Pieter de Hooch and Jan Vermeer. Nowadays every new house and flat has a wide picture window, in which, at night, the curtains are always drawn back. It is as if those within desperately want their neighbors to know nothing depraved and awful is going on. It may also be that those inside want to be able to look out and keep an eye on their neighbors. (Before the picture window, the Dutch had invented the *spiegeltje*, or little mirror, which was fastened to the outside window frame and allowed people inside the house, even upstairs, to keep an eye on goings-on down in the street.) In answer to a querulous letter I wrote while living in a Randstad apartment, I got a sympathetic reply from a Dutch couple, old friends of mine who now live in Paris but who had lived for a year in Osdorp. Jan, the husband, wrote: "What affected me most was the sense of all life being public and the routine of seeing people do the same things daily: flick out the tablecloth at the same hour, different women from different balconies doing the same thing. They would wash the windows and shake out the mop, woman by woman. Seeing, as you look out, everyone having the same sort of closet on the same sort of balcony for the same mops and buckets, and the same-sized garbage cans—it was like living in a modern prison with picture windows. I think they are an architectural and religious tic with us, these picture windows. We're trying to prove that we never belt our children or jump into bed with our wives. In Osdorp they might as well take the mattresses and use them to pad the paper-thin walls. Marieke's parents came one night to baby-sit—they come from Zeeland originally and hadn't believed our complaints about noise. Well, they heard every word of an argument that went on downstairs and every other word of the sermon that was on TV upstairs and the children crying next door and in the concrete staircase a man, drunk and belching, and out on the balcony someone ringing and ringing the next door bell. Her parents went home converted."

In our own case, in a much smaller building in Katwijk, we quickly came to appreciate the remark, "Your floor is my ceiling," which has been used as a refrain in a documentary film about modern Rotterdam. Our floor was our landlord's ceiling. What we had previously considered "normal healthy noise" from our children, the landlord took as evidence that his upstairs flat was being taken apart. We had no proper front door. Instead there was at the top of the stairs a sliding door, which left room on the stair-landing for a teak chest and allowed the bedroom opening off the landing to be considered separate premises that the landlord could, generously, lend to us or rent separately. The sliding door allowed all this and infuriated me. If pushed slowly, it closed with a whine. If pushed briskly, it rocked the house with a loud slam. The children found it hard to open and close. Left slightly open it allowed all the noise and cooking smells from downstairs to come in. Pretty soon we began pestering our children to keep quiet while they were in and trying to keep them outside as much as possible. The local schools were full, overcrowded, and had no room for transients. The baby got picked up whenever she began to cry. The fact that we were in a seaside town in April and the raw wind blew daily and damply from the North Sea didn't improve matters. We began to come down with all sorts of ailments, which the genial young local doctor kindly refrained from calling psychosomatic, but for which he prescribed archaic, pre-Randstad remedies: in the case of one real or imagined bug of mine, having to drink three liters of herb tea a day.

When I recovered (and herb tea worked wonders), I decided to find out a little more about the effect of apartment life on the Dutch. To begin with, I found that my local doctor's reluctance to use antibiotics was common. Aspirin is regarded with suspicion by many Dutch. Per capita, Holland consumes less drugs than any other country in Europe—a third of what the Germans and French consume. But they seem to have no such reservations about tranquillizers. Our doctor's wife said, "Oh, Henk prescribes them for all the women in the new apartments." Dr. Querido—who suggested that, while there were no presently ascertainable physical factors limiting population density, there might be psychological factors —said that he commonly used tranquillizers himself. I came across government reports mentioning "flat neurosis." (In our case, the symptoms of this were screaming at each other in whispers, and high fevers which refused to register on the thermometer.) I read a survey made in Pendrecht among the inhabitants of four hundred centrally heated flats, with balconies and elevators, in buildings seven to twelve stories high. Seventy-one per cent of the families with children fourteen and under would have liked to move. They didn't like the wind, the noise, and the lack of freedom for children to play safely and without annoying other people.

At this time I went to see H. Fiedeldy Dop, an Amsterdam pediatrician (Dutch: *kinderarts*) and translator of Dr. Benjamin Spock's *Baby and Child Care*. Dr. Fiedeldy Dop—whose euphonious name makes even the Dutch giggle—runs three social guidance clinics for children. He is on the board of an experimental action group called New Ways of Living, some of whose architect members I later talked to. He had worked in the new Amsterdam developments and was conscious of the great need and priority for roofs and shelter. Yet he believed that these developments had sprung from already obsolete thinking, fashionable before the Second World War with the Dutch members of the European architectural group

C.I.A.M., that towns could best be divided into a part where you work, a part where you live, and a part where you play. So these new developments began as dormitories. The men, the heads of the households, went away every morning and came back late every night. The women didn't have enough to do or to interest them. They were generally a long way from their mothers. They had mysterious stomach aches and headaches. They had few friends and they didn't find the shops very interesting and they would have liked to go to the old center of Amsterdam every afternoon if they could have arranged it. Father, coming home, hadn't a place of his own where he could read or a workshop where he could tinker. An infant, with no room of its own, got too much attention. "Babies need a chance to use their vocal chords," said Dr. Fiedeldy Dop, who talks rapidly, precisely, and has a keen edge of good humor. "They need to cry. Toddlers need to rush around. They have strong, aggressive emotions. They like noise, and in these apartments they aren't allowed to make any because of the elderly couple downstairs who start beating on the heating pipes just as you've put the toddler to bed and he's fallen asleep."

In the new developments Dr. Fiedeldy Dop found that the parents of young children were often in a rattled state, which he attributed partly to the fact that "there's no privacy—the flats are anti-sex." But it was children who really suffered. The small ones often didn't sleep well; they had nightmares in which they worked off some of the emotional energy they didn't have a chance to use during the day. There were no dark, private corners where they could hide, and if they made a mess, it was seen at once and at once cleaned up by mother. In their first years at school, children from these flats were often poor at arithmetic. They had no feeling for space and distance, or for the relation between things. The higher the flat in a block, the more plastic toys a child had and the fewer made of wood. Wood, which has been alive, which has grain and texture, makes more noise. In places where the apartment front doors have stupidly all been painted the same color, children often get lost. As for older children, there are no quiet places for them to do their homework. They get sent out in the street but there's not much to do except hang around. Dutch television doesn't come on until ten to seven at night, and after that is often pretty earnest. It wasn't surprising to hear from Dr. Fiedeldy Dop that Dutch children weren't fond of it and in winter —since the TV was in the living room and they had nowhere else to be and nothing else to do—they escaped from it all by going to bed.

❦ 4 ❦

DR. FIEDELDY DOP in some respects represents a change that has occurred in Holland in recent years in the way of looking at children, in seeing that children might *have* problems rather than simply *be* a problem. In their passion for clean and tidy houses, Dutch housewives have traditionally shooed their progeny into the streets where they could do everything they weren't allowed to do at home. In the seventeenth century, foreigners complained about Dutch children forming mobs which attacked passersby. In the nineteenth century, visiting British yachtsmen said the only trouble with Holland was the bands of small boys standing on bridges and canal banks from which they hurled lumps of mud and stones. One day, walking along the Beethovenstraat in Amsterdam, I was surrounded by a ring of little girls who began to dance around me, chanting what was clearly an exceptionally rude song. I wondered how I was to break out of the ring without hurting the little dears. People stopped and laughed at my embarrassment, and seemed rather disappointed when one child ran into a candy shop and left a gap in the circle through which I escaped. In Katwijk we were often followed by troops of small boys, yelling insults, and they were only put off by our most resolute refusal to recognize their presence. I visited one well-to-do household where the younger son was brought in to be introduced and with wild unruly laughter refused to honor us in that way; his mother said proudly, "He's a real Dutch boy." One older girl, babysitting for us, was surprised to hear that I hadn't insured my children against the risk that they might break somebody's picture window. All Dutch children were so insured by their parents, she said.

Jean-Nicholas Parival, who was professor of French at

Leiden University in the mid-seventeenth century, noted, "It is partly from this excessive indulgence [of Dutch parents] towards their children that there results the disorder which is often to be seen in their conduct. It is nevertheless surprising that there is not more disorder than there is, and there is perhaps no better proof of the natural goodness of the inhabitants of this country and the excellence of their disposition." There certainly does come a point when the boorish, mischievous child turns into a responsible adult—a bit constrained and repressed in appearance, but in no way suggesting that he might be easily cowed or bullied, the way a permissively brought-up child often seems to be as an adult, and the way the Dutch neighbors, the Germans, have been. Other elements in the Dutch environment may firm them up.

In one respect, however, they don't change. Noisy Dutch boys become noisy Dutch adolescents barreling down confined streets on unsilenced motorcycles, and a little later they seem to become noisy Dutch jet fighter pilots, brushing over the fields and cities at Mach 1, shaking in one long swoop all the picture windows from Enkhuizen to Bergen-op-zoom. Noise is one modern, urban problem that Holland is well endowed with. Dutch demographers call Holland the European Manhattan, and in respect of decibels the description is fair. The small size of the country may be why planes seem to fly lower there: coming in to land on the Belgian border in the southwest a plane may have started descending on the northeastern frontier with Germany. The holding pattern for Schiphol, the international airport just outside Am-

sterdam, covers half the Randstad. (The elementary
school at Badhoevedorp, near Schiphol, is experimenting
with earphones for its pupils.) But one also suspects that
the Dutch have got used to the strafing effect of low-fly-
ing planes and to the constant roar and bang; in no country does one so often hear sonic booms. Perhaps the Dutch
are adjusted to more noise—rows of facing houses form
echo chambers, and the ground shakes easily. Pile-driving
equipment thuds all day in the Randstad. Trucks rumble
heavily over the paved streets. Buildings quiver. Most
noisy of all is the *bromfiets*—at the last count in 1966
there were 1,578,200 of them in Holland, and there are
more daily, as the swing from pedal-powered bicycles to
these small motorcycles continues. In Utrecht, for instance, more than one hundred and eighty people per
thousand over sixteen years of age own a *bromfiets* or
brommer. In the age group just over sixteen, *brommer*-
owning is advertised by a display of primitive mechanical skill. The first thing to do with a new *brommer*
is to strip the guts out of the silencer, so that flat-out
at thirty mph over the *kinderhoofdjes* it sounds as
much as possible like a Hawker Hunter at five hundred feet cracking the sound barrier. However, rules
and regulations are gradually coming into existence, in
some places with a strong will to enforce them as *brommers* increase. The Groningen police have been confiscat-
ing *brommers* on the second offense, and the Delft police
can take any *brommer* which has been altered in any part
or specification since leaving the factory. In some towns
brommers are banned on certain streets at certain hours.

On the Boulevard along the seafront at Katwijk they are
banned every evening from seven to midnight.

Throughout the urban world, noise is now being recognized as more than a nuisance. (Noise in the average
North American home has more than doubled in the last
forty years, and a recent study in Detroit suggested that
men exposed to large amounts of noise suffered more
cold, influenza, and infection.) In Holland, specialists for
some time past have thought of noise as a social evil,
threatening mental and bodily health and—a real prod
to action—causing economic damage. A place where research into noise is being conducted is T.N.O., the Dutch
Institute for Applied Scientific Research at Delft. T.N.O.
was founded with government aid in 1930 and now, with
grants from government and industry, employs more than
four thousand people. One of its sixty constituent bodies
is the Research Institute for Public Health Engineering. I
spent a morning at this institute's Sound and Light
Department, whose director, Mr. J. van den Eijk, told me
about some of the work he and his colleagues were doing.
One area they were interested in was industrial deafness
—an aspect of life in shipyards and mills which had been
recognized for a long time without much effort to dis-
cover at what point workers were seriously affected. "In
America the feeling in the past has been that if a worker
keeps most speech intelligibility it is all right. We are a
little more perfectionist," said Mr. van den Eijk. "A small
loss of hearing may seem insignificant at the time, but
since people naturally lose more hearing as they get older,
they really can't afford to lose any. And there are so many

sounds you can easily lose—the natural sound of birds, or the sound of a flute. We've learned, moreover, that it isn't just deafness you can acquire working as a riveter's mate—you may get high blood pressure from the noise as well. We have been working to collect as much data as possible so that we know how much hearing is lost with so much noise. From there we can go on to test means of protecting hearing. We can train men to protect themselves. And we can work at obtaining the cooperation of industry. Formerly, industrial companies complained that audiometers costing fifteen hundred guilders were expensive, but they now realize that the loss of work days is more expensive. The attitude of workers is changing, too. In the old days, for a shipyard worker being deaf was a real badge of merit—it showed he'd served his time. Nowadays the young men don't want to work in a deafening place."

(This is perhaps a good moment to mention one cheerful note in the world of industrial noise. At Enschede Printers in Haarlem, where the presses rolling out bank notes and postage stamps make an earsplitting clatter, the firm uses the sound of a bugle blown over the loudspeaker system to call executives to the telephone.)

In the construction of modern apartments and houses, as I had already experienced, Dutch builders, like those elsewhere, have saved money when it came to insulation. "What we're told," said Mr. van den Eijk, "is that people will get used to noise. People will get used to the sonic booms of the SST. I think this is wrong. We have to choose what are the good things and the bad things developed by science and technology. Should we all take LSD just because it has been invented? With noise, it's not just a question of cutting it down afterward. A lot of damage can be avoided by taking it into account at the planning stage. A lot of unhappiness in the southern development of Amsterdam, Buitenveldert, could have been forestalled by not placing it downwind of the new extension of the Schiphol runways. Here in Delft, highrise apartments have been built fifty meters from a busy highway, and then trees have been planted to try and cure the problem, as if trees were magic anti-noise things. In that respect, I saw the other day the design for a new development of shops, created in such a way that there would be a constant whirlwind there. It would be the last place you would go to shop. Every time you did you would lose your hat. We told them about it. It isn't just a good-looking environment you have to create. You have to take nature and building physics into account."

Mr. van den Eijk and his colleagues have done research into sound prevention in buildings and are now working on getting across to builders and architects the results of their research. Architects tend to react in a surly fashion to this sort of advice. It is one more technical restraint on their freedom. Builders see it as one more addition to building costs, and their common answer to complaints about apartment noise is to tell the tenant to install thick carpeting.

In fact, I learned at T.N.O. that a floor (which is also a ceiling) has to be either heavy or complicated to retard the transmission of noise. In terms of expense, a simple, thick, and heavy floor, with more concrete and less steel, need cost no more than a thinner, lighter floor, with more steel and less concrete. But particularly effective against noise is a so-called floating floor. This involves a main concrete floor, on top of which lies a one-centimeter-thick layer of glass wool, on top of which is poured another four-centimeter layer of concrete. T.N.O. after a big fight got this into the Dutch Building Code in 1960. A visual-aid book was then designed and distributed to architects and builders. The press, radio, and television were enlisted to publicize the problems of noise and to help persuade government ministers, state departments, and municipal authorities. "As a scientist, I'm reluctant to get involved in that sort of effort," Mr. van den Eijk said. "One feels the facts should speak for themselves. But nowadays there are so many facts. They often don't get brought to the attention of the people who have to make the decisions. So science and public education with the help of the communications media have to go together. In Holland it also helps if we let out that the Germans are ahead of us in some branch of research, as they often are. Anyway, we have done surveys and calculations in Rotterdam and Amsterdam to find out about the cost of sound insulation. We calculated the cost of floating floors, sound insulation in communal staircases, and thicker walls between apartments. We found that the additional cost per week in the rent of each apartment so improved would be one guilder fifty cents—that is about forty American cents, the price of a pack of cigarettes, far less than the weekly cost of a television set."

Other T.N.O. scientists have helped to muffle the

chainsaws of lumberjacks and have designed soundproof boxes for the noisy compressors which are stationed at intervals on the natural-gas pipelines from the rich gas fields recently discovered near Groningen (probably the biggest single natural gas field in the world). A T.N.O. physicist has invented a machine that will program the complete thermal behavior of a proposed building. Also in the field of research, I was interested to learn that Philips, the giant Dutch industrial electronic company, which has a reputation for successful experimentation, many years ago bought the rights to the American-invented Erikson steam engine and now, after having done a great deal of sophisticated work on it, have been asked by General Motors to develop it as a possible motor for small American cars. There is a story, whose truth I won't swear to, that a recent party of Japanese scientists touring the Philips plant at Eindhoven were allowed to take as many photographs as they liked while walking round, but in the lobby, as they were leaving, hidden infrared beams exposed their films.

❦ 5 ❦

ASPECTS OF CLAUSTROPHOBIA.

"I couldn't breathe," said Ottilie, the opera singer in the 1906 novel *Old People and the Things That Pass*, by Louis Couperus, explaining why she left Holland to live in France. "The grey skies hindered my breathing, and the houses stopped me from producing my voice properly. I had to expand my lungs."

"Here in the west of Holland," said Mr. Thomas Hoog, as I looked at the private bulb fields he has managed to preserve within the city of Haarlem, "we walk always between barbed wire."

"It would seem," said Dr. Querido, talking to an Amsterdam conference on World Population and Mental Health, "that a human society at a given moment is an expression of an equilibrium—a balance struck between the amount of comfort to be obtained from fellow members, and the discomforts arising from the same source."

"I went abroad," said Mr. Ivo Blom, a Rotterdam city official, as we sat drinking in a smoky bar, "I went looking for sunshine and space. I sat on a hot Corsican hillside. There was a deserted village, no people, a view of the sea. Paradise! All that room! I thought, I will retire here. But then a week later I came back over the van Brienenoord Bridge at rush hour in the rain and saw Rotterdam and knew that I would never live for long anywhere else. There are things here I could not do without."

The curious thing is that although many people in Holland claim to be bothered by more cars on the roads, big classes in the schools, no room in the universities, and an ever-more-crowded future (so much so that some say they will send their children to live in Norway or Australia, or vote for an extra tax on families with more than three children), many more are sanguine. The majority perhaps had a spokesman in the lady who was asked on a

Dutch radio program if she were horrified by the prospect of overcrowding. She replied, "Oh no. I think it gets cosier and cosier. More families, more birthdays."

The Dutch lead close lives in which the family matters. Letters are generally addressed not to Mr. and Mrs. Spinoza but to the Family Spinoza. Birthday calendars, reminding one of responsibilities to all one's relations, hang on the back of the toilet door, where one can't fail to brood about what one should send to Cousin Willy or Aunt Bien. There is a Dutch term, *familie-ziekte*, family sickness, for describing the condition of a person over-conscious of what the young Indian sociologist K. Ishwaran calls "the kinship system and its obligations." Among the families of Leiden University students, Ishwaran found people who were proud of fulfilling family duties and attending family functions but protested all the while that they weren't family-sick. Indeed, many people in Holland seem capable of relating in detail the lives of distant relatives. When the Dutch say goodbye to someone, they also ask to be remembered to all of his family—not knowing the names, they are liable to prolong the goodbye until they have been told what other members of the family they need to be remembered to. In Dutch, this family can be split into the *gezin*, which is the immediate family circle of mother, father, and children, and the *familie*, which is the wider network of grandparents, uncles, aunts, cousins, etc. But though urbanization seems to isolate and stress the self-importance of the *gezin*, this conjugal family maintains strong ties with the family at large. Bad times are a binding force. In the hunger winter of 1944–45, urban families were grateful for every food-growing rural relative they could muster. And the most cosmopolitan Dutchman will make a point of driving home for his mother's birthday, or arrange to take his father for a week's holiday every summer.

These days in the Randstad, families have fewer children. Divorce is three or four times higher in the Randstad than it is in the rest of the country. This, one might quickly say, reflects urban morals. On the other hand, there is the point of view expressed by Joseph L. Blau of Columbia University in the *American Quarterly* (Winter 1957): "The lower incidence of divorce in rural areas is evidence of a lower moral standard there, a standard that permits all manner of aggressive acts by mate against mate, provided the aggression and violation takes place within the holy bounds of matrimony. It is immoral narrowness and bigotry that compels people who hate each other to continue in 'holy deadlock' in order to satisfy the obsolete ethical standards of their rural neighbors." In fact, although urbanization goes on, the divorce rate in Holland has remained fairly steady for the last six years. (Most men and women get divorced late in Holland, after ten to nineteen years of marriage.) One reason for the strength of the Dutch family may be that, despite legal emancipation, Dutch women play their major role at home. Women make up only about a quarter of the total labor force, the same proportion reported in the 1889 census. Only 3 per cent of married women work, a figure which can be compared with 26 per cent in America, 27 per cent in England, and 32 per cent in

Germany. At home, the Dutch woman runs a tight ship—
the Dutch husband, like the admiral of the fleet, leaves
the running of the vessel he is aboard to the ship's captain. Washing up, shopping, or even cleaning the shoes
are not his affair. A young filmmaker I met in Rotterdam
told me that, as a child, he rarely saw his father during
the week—if he did come home early he buried himself
in a paper or book, and had nothing to do with what was
going on in the home. In middle age the Dutch husband
looks a lot younger than his wife. Lithe Dutch girls
seem quickly to become powerful, big-bosomed matrons,
thick-waisted, full of household responsibilities. In fact,
Dutchmen seem to marry girls who rapidly become their
mothers, which may be one reason the men retain their
boyish looks. Certainly sex and marriage seem to have
little to do with each other for a Dutchman. One French
observer claims, perhaps patriotically, that Dutchmen go
to Paris for their "light relief." Amsterdam and most
other large cities have streets where the men can prowl
around and examine the *kippetjes* sitting in their picture
windows—nicely arranged still-lives of false-eyelashed,
mascaraed women with their skirts pulled up high, sitting
reading letters or doing their nails while waiting for cus-
tomers. But one wonders if the men ever go in. A recent
Spanish ambassador, the Duke de Baena, quotes someone
he cautiously calls "a South American colleague, a great
admirer of Dutch women," who believed that the whole
drama of Dutch life was that the women had very warm
temperaments, but were tied to men with cool or tepid
natures.

In some ways a matriarchy of the Dutch kind makes

for a more private world, and the increasingly urban middle-class nature of life contributes to this. The rural Dutch family and the working class family in the past lived with wide-open doors. But in the crowded modern city, privacy is more important—you don't want to know everybody; strangers should remain strangers. Friends don't call to visit without telephoning first, or waiting for an invitation. There seems to be a kind of deviousness that is a by-product of living in a large and crowded place where too many social demands can be made on you. It becomes difficult to be honest. There are white lies used to get out of engagements or put things off. The protocol of crowdedness is a deceit by which you attempt to protect your independence, and of course family obligations are an excellent excuse. J. Goudsblom of the University of Amsterdam writes (in a sociological study called *Dutch Society*), "The conjugal family should live a life of its own, in a separate house with an independent income, enjoying a proper measure of privacy and autonomy. When the housing shortage forces a newlywed couple to move in with a parental family, this is regarded as prompted by emergency* and is viewed as an infringement upon the norm that each family should have its own home."

The "norm" is reflected in Dutch fiction. Dutch novels are family novels or—a sign of the same preoccupation—

---

* It may well be prompted by an emergency. In a study done by G. A. Kooy and M. Keuls, called *Enforced Marriage in the Netherlands*, it is reckoned that in 16 per cent of all Dutch marriages (which took place in the period 1959–61), the first child was born within seven months of the wedding ceremony. [A.B.]

antifamily novels, in which the hero is an outsider. *Old People and the Things That Pass*, by Louis Couperus, is a brilliant depiction of the thick, internecine family life of The Hague at the turn of the century. Anna Blaman's *Carolus* also does an excellent job, Dutch readers say, of portraying "the stifling closeness of Dutch bourgeois life." The other aspect, the rebellion from this closeness, is to be seen in Arthur van Schendel's (1874–1946) *The Waterman*—though it is a muted, almost desperately inarticulate rebellion—and in the works of the contemporary Dutch novelist Willem Hermans (b. 1921), whose very language seems to be used as a whip against Dutch middle-class life and conventions. One Dutch critic has described Hermans's characters as "involved in trying to rid themselves of libidinous desires which tie them to mother and sister, while at the same time they labor under a father's oppression." Holland, one might add, is pre-eminently a country of readers. More books are published there per capita than anywhere else in the world. When the family gathers in the living room, people put their heads into books and find privacy.

The piece of furniture in that living room I find most interesting is the *kabinet*—perhaps an antique handed down from an ancestral home, or a reproduction of an old piece, part chest, part tallboy. These *kabinets* are like the seventeenth- and eighteenth-century houses on the Vecht, the expression of the taste and wealth of the Dutch burgher aristocracy. Today the aristocracy is no more, the burghers are numerous, and the bourgeoisie (whose ideals and aspirations have been in many ways influenced by that burgher way of life) encompasses almost the entire nation. Maybe those ideals are clung to all the more firmly because of the speed with which circumstances are changing. One has the impression that where life is suddenly shaped in a new, rather inflexible mold, people hang on all the harder to "the old way of life"—that, indeed, such clinging may be therapeutic for those unable to make, say, a speedy adjustment to life in a flat in a new development, where they have less privacy and less contact with their relatives. Old-fashioned furniture is popular, and so is old gin, old cheese, old buildings, and old boats. Young people go to fashionable weddings in antique horse-drawn carriages. The royal family (which young republicans say is obsolete, of no use) receives vast affection, with thousands of people going personally on the Queen's birthday to Soestdijk Palace to present Juliana with a bouquet of flowers. And in the new land of the IJsselmeer polders, prefabricated modern farm buildings rise in traditional shapes and styles.

The pressure of the past, of course, can be claustrophobic for some: all the detritus of the revolt against Spain, Calvinism, windmills, wooden shoes, fingers in the dike, even Rembrandt and tulips form a traditional burden that many would—at least once in a while—like to cast off, together with the bourgeois ideals which seem to enclose Holland in a thick, complacent fug. But the virtues of this "highest manifestation" of a middle-class civilization can be too easily mocked. One might, more generously, note that in this bourgeois world education counts high—a survey made in the 1950's indicated that the Dutch put university professors at the top of the

social ladder. In a list of fifty-seven occupations, they
preceded physicians, mayors of cities, judges, and engineers. Way back in ninth place were directors of large
companies. To the usual pejorative connotation of bourgeois, the Dutch add the notions of anxiety, forethought,
conservation, and self-sacrifice. They are responsible—not
just in appearance, like the young men and women you
see in shops and railway stations, dressed up like respect-
able middle-aged, middle-class couples—but in spirit.
One of the most interesting aspects of *Provo*, the Dutch
movement which was among the first and brightest of
radical movements of the last decade, was that it
blossomed forth with a number of responsible civic ideas.
Provo (which I mean to look at in more detail later) also
helped to enlarge a mood in which things bourgeois were
not always treated earnestly, soberly, and complacently.
You expect to see lace curtains, even in the windows of
barges, but not as I did one day, neatly drawn apart, in
the back window of a psychedelically painted Citroen
2 c.v.

One aspect of Dutch domestic life that exasperated
me, now and then to the point of wanting to kick plant
pots over or throw mud around, was the cleanliness—or,
to make an immediate distinction, all the cleaning, scrub-
bing, dusting, carpet-banging, and sweeping that goes on.
In the seventeenth century Sir William Temple was told
the story of a burgomaster who knocked at the door of a
bourgeois home. He told the servant who came that he
wanted to speak to her mistress. The servant, however,
noticed a bit of mud on his shoes, and not letting him
step through the door, or say another word, she picked

him up, flung him across her shoulders, marched across two rooms, and then dumped him at the foot of the stairs. There she removed his shoes, got him some slippers, and said, finally, "The mistress will be pleased to see you." Sir William thought that the root cause of this manic behavior was the crowdedness of the country. "The extreme moisture of the Air, I take to be the occasion of the great neatness in their Houses, and cleanliness in their Towns. For without the help of those Customs, their Country would not be habitable by such crowds of People, but the Air would corrupt upon every Hot Season, and expose the Inhabitants to general and infectious Diseases." Johan Huizinga attributed it as a national characteristic to the need for absolutely germ-free conditions in cheese-making. But the fact is that while Dutch houses have always been kept spotless, the Dutch themselves have not. "We are not a particularly clean people," said Dr. Querido. "In the past the emphasis has been on exterior appearances rather than personal hygiene."

One of the interesting effects of urbanization is a change in this emphasis. Dutch women are shaving under their arms, and using deodorants. The streets, however, are no longer immaculate: street cleaners are hard to find and street-sweeping machines are impeded by parked cars. Old cars—even old, dependable Dutch Dafs —have to be dumped somewhere, and from motorways you can see scrap heaps in the corners of meadows, though a little better hedged or fenced than in other countries. (These car dumps are generally run by gypsies; yesterday's nomadic tinkers have become the sedentary scrap-metal merchants of today.) From cars driving along

Dutch highways paper cups and candy wrappers fly forth onto the roadsides. One day at Oostmahoorn, in Friesland, I saw a young woman accompanied by a child bring four pails of garbage out of a café, walk down the steep, stone-faced dike, and tip the refuse into the Lauwerszee. Tin cans sank, the gulls swooped to pick up what was edible, and a great deal in the form of plastic bags and paper cartons floated off on the tide. Many glass jars and bottles bought in Dutch grocery stores require a deposit paid on them, what the Dutch call a *statiegeld*— in a week's groceries it might come to a ransom of at least fifty U.S. cents, so it is worth taking the bottles back for the refund. But now, slowly, "no deposit, no return" containers are making an appearance. Plastic and paper produce proportionate litter. One looks with sudden pleasure at signs of the old national obsession. In the courtyard of a *hofje*, or square of old people's homes, near Leeuwarden, there was a swallow's nest under an archway, and on the stone pavement directly beneath the nest a cardboard box had been placed to catch the droppings.

The Dutch do not seem to be a spontaneous people. In fact, today they give the impression of being a little studied, as if they had something on their minds they can't or don't want to express. The Duke de Baena writes, "I must say in honesty that I have met more nervous individuals in Holland than anywhere else." Where restlessness is hard to remedy (and it is curious how fond such a superficially stolid people seem to be of the word *onrust*, which means "unrest"—they use it to name houses, sandbanks, boats, and restaurants) and where privacy is in short supply, life grows more intense. There may be a sign of this in the hitherto excellent Dutch life-expectancy rate, which in recent years has leveled out. The Ministry of Social Affairs and Public Health is cautious about some aspects of the Dutch health situation, mentioning as reasons for this "the high rate of absenteeism due to illness, the rapidly increasing mortality figures due to cancer (particularly among men), the increasing mortality rate due to heart and vascular diseases and the strikingly increasing number of cases of heart trouble among younger people, and the increasing number of people seriously injured and killed in traffic accidents"—all, one might say, urban complaints. Dr. Querido told me that he considered one of the most important features of Dutch preventive medicine to be research into early symptoms of coronary attacks. It was to be hoped that GP's would soon have the knowledge by which they could recognize that a man was liable to have a heart attack, and could then send him to bed for two weeks to avoid it. Dr. Querido added, "I don't think people are cracking up as a result of overcrowding. At least, if they are, there is something else already wrong with them. But I think one does see an increased irritability. It's evident in the thwarted aggressiveness on the roads everywhere, not just in Holland. You can't choose your own speed all the time. You want to open up, but can't. However, our violence rate is low,* our alcoholism rate is low, and there doesn't

---

* On Dutch crime: In 1965 there were twelve murder convictions. Sexual offenses, thefts, and "destructive" crimes are roughly what they have been over the past five years. The only category to show a steady rise is traffic offenses. The suicide rate is steady—presently 1.3 per 1,000 people.

seem to be any general tendency here to accept war as a
political solution to any problem—in fact, perhaps even
the reverse."

For all that, life is intense in Holland, in feeling and in
fact. A Dutch farmer is used to getting a yield of eleven
thousand kilos of wheat from a hectare of land—an
American farmer gets on the average an equivalent yield
of eleven hundred kilos. The speed of change and growth
is such that expansion that once took a century now takes
ten years. Everything being flat makes everything seem
nearer. All the digging, and damming, and diking that
goes on sometimes seems to be in itself a form of escape
—a way of staying so active and busy one doesn't notice
more and more people closer and closer together being
equally busy. The proximity of things occasionally turns
into a fierce pressure. Although the Dutch don't seem
spontaneous and believe that they never rob trains or
blow anything up, they have their explosions. In 1966 a
pyromaniac terrorized the section of Amsterdam around
the Zeedijk and the Nieuwmarkt, stuffing gasoline-
soaked rags through mail-slots in front doors and then
throwing in a lighted match. Two out of three Dutch
girls we had babysitting for us had constant anxieties
about being followed by strange men, and one girl absolutely refused to travel in trains, except during rush
hours, for fear of sharing a compartment with a lone
man, undoubtedly a sex fiend. When a rather heavy-
handed Dutch satirical television program did a skit
showing a man saying the Lord's Prayer to a TV set,
rather than to the Almighty, there was an eruption of

outraged calls and letters—mainly anonymous—to the station, denouncing the blasphemy. One letter-writer threatened to rape the girl announcer. (But immediately —perhaps demonstrating that such opportunities don't come often enough—a team of Dutch sociologists began a study of the explosion.) The best-selling author in Holland today is Jan Cremer, whose banal and boring fantasies of blood and sex seem to have struck a responsive note in the Dutch. In the fall of 1967, nearly three hundred thousand people came to the town of 's-Hertogenbosch, in North Brabant, to an exhibition of the works of the painter Hieronymus Bosch (c. 1450–1516), who was, before Goya, the most brilliant illustrator of man's nastiest habits and imaginings. Carel van Mander wrote in his *Schilderboek*, published in Haarlem in 1604, "How pleasant and natural he was with flames and burning, and fire and smoke."

To anyone used to looser, more expansive places, there are times when Holland is impossible. There were days in Katwijk when the sliding door at the entrance to our apartment, perhaps rocking a little in the draft, signaled to me the tight-fisted, cramped character of the people, and if a *brommer* went shrieking down the street or the woman next door came out on her balcony and began to beat a carpet for the third time since breakfast, I would start to shout in simple fury. My wife would say, "Go for a walk, and take some of the children." But at such times the constant, nagging wind would be blowing sand inland from the beach, and big trucks would be bringing it back again, and around the duck pond in the little park I would notice a single rusty strand of barbed wire hung at exactly the height of the eyes of a three-year-old child.

I claim to be a fairly placid person, but Holland sometimes made me feel I was a manic-depressive. For the depression would lift (and perhaps the weather and atmospheric pressure had something to do with it), and be replaced on the next mild day by an intense enthusiasm, assembled out of shafts of light, falling into rooms or onto that level landscape from billowing stacks of cloud. A bridge would lift to let a barge pass through, and a child would wave to another child. Walking down a scrubby lane in the Veluwe, I would suddenly come across a dense, quietly stirring field of rye, white-green like Dürer's grasses. Sometimes in an oil refinery and sometimes in a city street I would realize that, although one has intense depressions in Holland, one also has more moments of intense exhilaration than one has elsewhere.

❧ 6 ❧

THERE ARE TWO BASIC WAYS to escape from the crowded city—you go further out or you turn further in. People with houses and apartments they don't particularly like are perhaps the first to flee—either to the more various attractions of the historic center of cities, or to parks, recreation areas, and foreign countries. They may even just go out and drive. The information officer of the Amsterdam Department of Public Works told me that he always stayed at home at weekends, the roads were too crowded. But then, he had a seventeenth-century house on a canal in the old city, and a walled garden to which the sounds of traffic barely penetrated. Dr. Querido told me that he thought the real horrors of an overcrowded society were in fact to be found for the most part in modern travel—in the sausage-factory atmosphere of airline journeys, or on traffic-jammed autobahns where you were unable to choose your own speed. His answer, too, was to stay at home. But when you stayed at home you wanted an agreeable, comfortable, private place where—spending perhaps as much money as you would on travel—you could have paintings, music, books, friends, and silence.

This turning in, this traveling in the interior, is something the Dutch have learned to do even in unpropitious circumstances. One feels that in the most public of worlds, they have discovered how to get wrapped up in themselves. I have passed houses at night and looked in, as one is encouraged to look in through those uncurtained windows, to see the head of the household seated in a self-created pool of privacy, sometimes not reading the paper or book before him, not smoking the pipe in his hand or sipping the gin on the table, cut off as if with the thickest of curtains from his wife sewing or his children reading—simply sitting with his head on one hand, staring and thinking. If you could get round in

front and look into his eyes, you might see that look,
fixed on a point halfway between you and himself, which
Rembrandt painted in his great self-portraits, the look of
a man staring at himself in a mirror or in the mirror of
his own mind, the look of someone trying to find an
answer to the question of how to balance the two demands of life—the demand of possessions, of the need
to acquire and then look after *things*; and the demand of
ideas, of the spirit, of all the insubstantial daydreams
one needs to give time to, even if it is but as a never-
ending brooding on the question: What am I doing here?

To me, being by myself means being in a room alone.
The Dutch, like children from big families, can be by
themselves in a room with six other people or on a canal
bank lined with people fishing, almost shoulder to
shoulder. Stand on any street corner in Amsterdam at
5:30 in the evening and watch the phalanxes of bicycles
go by—a sight not quite what it used to be, but still
impressive enough. If you pick at random one serenely
pedaling individual from the thick, staggered formation,
you see that he isn't really looking at the city, the street,
or the other bicyclists around him. He seems aware only
of a small portion of space, a bubble within which he and
his bike exist with a few spare inches outside his knuckles
on the handlebars, his twirling feet, his steady shoulders.
He is secure within this space which encloses him and
moves with him, the way energy moves through water,
giving an appearance of fast forward motion to a wave.
Then the traffic light has changed, he is gone, and
others have whirled up to the junction, jousting with

each other in a remote, impersonal way, ignoring an interloping car or a sputtering *bromfiets*. On each face— the face of a girl, the face of a dignified gentleman wearing a hat—you may glimpse the most private of smiles. Pedaling homeward, they have their own thoughts as their wheels revolve and cars and trams and *brommers* assail them from four or even six directions, the man on the right, whatever his vehicle, having the right of way which he—sometimes with courage rather than sense— always takes, their reflexes operating splendidly though their minds are elsewhere. These Amsterdam rush-hour bicycles always move me. They are a wonder, like salmon going upstream, demonstrating as they do that in the most crowded places a human being can go on being himself—can become even more himself—and that, in such a place, if you pause for a moment, you can't help but be aware of it.

I have had such feelings in a place that seems even less conducive to contemplation, the Rijksmuseum on a sum- mer afternoon. There you realize what it is to live not only in a crowded country but in a country whose charms and achievements thousands of people from other countries want to see. It is ironic that peace, prosperity, and the age of leisure have done what Hitler's Reich did not, which is to enable the people of Germany to enjoy Holland as if it were theirs. In any event, early on a winter morning is a good time to look at pictures in the Rijksmueum. At other times you need to be well ad- justed to Randstad conditions, so that you can more or less close your ears to tour guides doling out anecdotes about a careful selection of notable paintings, and can stand the proximity of massive hausfraus and earnest college girls *doing* the museum without feeling (*a*) choked up, (*b*) hyper-aesthetic, and (*c*) generally outraged at the philistinism of the tourist-dominated world. If you aren't overmuch worried by these things, you may find it possible even in the season to look at and "get something" from Dutch art. In the packed little room where the Vermeers and de Hoochs hang—to which you have to fight your way through the crowds thronged before "The Night Watch"—I have seen a young man standing in front of the "Girl Reading a Letter," the Vermeer which is possibly the greatest painting in the world, standing oblivious to the buzzing, jostling mob with tears streaming down his face, he was so moved. And a Japanese girl, no feelings manifested, fixed in a kind of trance before "The Little Street." For ten minutes she was a rock around which the others in the room eddied, coming up and then rolling back as they came in contact with her concentration, which was also a communion. I felt that these two were drawing from Vermeer what Vermeer was offering. A. B. de Vries, the director of The Mauritshuis in The Hague, writes, "What distinguishes Vermeer from his contemporaries is the intensity of his observation. He can only have registered the basic structure of a wall, a bridge, a fence, roofs, and shutters by studying them intensely at close quarters. He must have looked long and often at the shifting play of sun and clouds in the sky, at the water in the canals rippled by the wind. No one in the Seventeenth Century had ever penetrated the substance of the visible world so deeply."

The visible world is still very much on hand in Holland, and the kind of trance that individuals fall into in the face of it seems to enable them sometimes to penetrate its surface and make, if not a work of art, then a state of mind or a perception. There is a general willingness to believe in the possibility of mysteries behind the facts. One detects an atmosphere in which the intensity of things may help make less usual kinds of perception possible. One is reminded of what in earlier times was called "weird," and taken for granted. With some of this in mind, I drove one day to Utrecht to see Professor W. H. C. Tenhaeff, director of the Parapsychology Institute of the State University in that city. Professor Tenhaeff was a jovial, bearded short man of seventy-four who for many years has been investigating what he calls "the personality structure of paragnosts"—paragnosts being individuals who appear to have telepathic powers and who seem particularly common in Holland. (The word comes from the Greek: *para*, beyond, *gnosis*, knowledge.) Writing about them, Professor Tenhaeff uses the word "gift" in careful quotation marks, and is fairly critical of the spiritualist and theosophical terminology such people tend to lean on, though he isn't prepared to throw all such props away. In Holland, many paragnosts work professionally, finding lost objects or missing persons. Some, acting as psychotherapists, listen for a small fee to a person's troubles and give advice—taking time doctors or specialists might feel they couldn't afford. A number, considering themselves "healers," go in for Mesmerism, following the practice of the Austrian physician F. A. Mesmer (1734–1815), who believed in the curative power—through "mineral magnetism"—of the laying-on of hands. (Having lunch in the Pavilion café on the island of Schiermonnikoog, I was told that the proprietor had cured many people in this way. He died of a tumor in 1969.) According to Professor Tenhaeff, most of these magnetizers are great quacks, but he thinks that they occasionally have a beneficial influence on the sick. He says, "Whether this influence should be attributed to a 'vital force' that goes out from them is so far unknown. What is certain is that one can find some remarkable suggestion-therapists among these individuals."

One such person was Greet Hofmans, who died in November 1968 at the age of seventy-three, a gaunt, masculine-looking woman who gave up work in a factory (following what she said was a call from God) twenty years or so ago and moved to the estate of Baron van Heeckeren van Molecaten. There she practiced "healing." Afflicted people came and recited their problems while Miss Hofmans held them by the arms and prayed for them. Many believed she helped them. Indeed, her reputation spread to the Dutch royal family, and having had little luck with orthodox medicine, Prince Bernhard brought Miss Hofmans to Soestdijk, hoping she might cure his daughter Princess Maria Christina, who had been partially blind from birth. This Miss Hofmans was unable to do. She blamed the lack of success on Prince Bernhard's lack of faith. She did, however, become the confidante of Queen Juliana, mother of the princess and wife of Bernhard. The Baron van Heeckeren van Molecaten became the Queen's private secretary. When, after several years, Prince Bernhard asked them to leave, Miss Hofmans and the Baron moved to the estate of the Queen Mother, Queen Wilhelmina. There was a great hullabaloo in 1956 when the Dutch press disclosed the relations between Miss Hofmans and the royal family. Queen Juliana had to give up seeing Miss Hofmans. The government then proceeded to investigate to see if Miss Hofmans had been practicing medicine illegally, but decided she hadn't, because she had never accepted a fee.

This episode confirmed many people in their belief that anything to do with paragnosts was dubious or bizarre. But despite this, and the uneasiness most people feel when faced with something that isn't readily comprehensible, there is a serious interest in such phenomena. The State University of Utrecht has been backing Professor Tenhaeff's researches since before the war. Paragnosts are often used by Dutch lawyers and police to find missing people, and bodies. A lawyer who was the uncle of a woman we met in Katwijk asked the well-known paragnost Gérard Croiset to help find a member of his own family. Over the telephone, Croiset described to the lawyer just where the girl was then in Rotterdam, what tram she was riding on, and what stop she got off at. The girl was found.

Many paragnosts grow up being regarded as "strange" by friends and family, and often seek the company of spiritualists in order to escape their feelings of difference. Spiritualist circles then impose on them a folklore and vocabulary which is anything but scientific, although Professor Tenhaeff has found they will sometimes do without it in the presence of an academic investigator. " 'They' and 'The Other Side,' " he says, "can be accepted as meaning 'oneself' and 'within.' " The professor believes that the guiding spirits or controls which mediums claim to have are probably a secondary personality of the medium that takes over in a state of trance. One such "occultist" refused to be investigated by the professor, having no desire, he said, to subject himself "to tests that had sprung from the brain of materialistically thinking psychologists." However, Professor Tenhaeff says nobly of another paragnost, who does a great deal of pseudo-scientific philosophizing, "Although Mr. X's system of metaphysics (in common with that of so many other paragnosts) bears the stamp of defective schooling, and of a lack of philosophical training, it nonetheless deserves attention as being what Jaspers calls *Kundgabe der Seele*, manifestation of the soul."

Professor Tenhaeff is the first to admit that his investigation is still at the beginning, with a few tentative judgments resting on the surface of an incomplete collection of data, and most of it has overtones of pigeonholes and categories that mean little except to the specialist conducting the tests (e.g., we are told that paragnosts generally lack "will," "aggressiveness," and "inner strength," and have "increased suggestibility connected with incomplete individuation"). The layman may perhaps then be pardoned for an interest in the trivia which seems to be connected with the "gift." Paragnosts often have images useful to women wanting to know if their husbands are "carrying on," or to men wanting to know if the girl they are thinking of marrying has an incurable disease. They can generally tell strangers their right names and where they met their wives. Gérard Croiset usually "sees" in black and white, but sometimes where necessary for orientation, in the case of something lost, the image has appeared to him in colors. In an article in the *International Journal of Neuropsychiatry*, Professor Tenhaeff notes the fact that Croiset, while being consulted over the telephone by a client, declared that a picture of a lighthouse with four windows had just appeared to him. "Under one of the windows he 'saw' two yellow stars, caused by rust. On checking, the picture proved to be correct."

Some unwitting paragnosts have got a real fright when they found that a prediction they have made, perhaps as a joke, has come true. One successful prediction Professor Tenhaeff is fond of came in the form of a "spontaneous olfactory hallucination." The paragnost in his own home smelled what he thought was a burning rubber gas tube, and told the professor he thought the Parapsychology Institute would catch fire. Two days later the convertor in an institute tape recorder short-circuited, overheated, and burned away the rubber coating on a wire. For several hours the rooms of the institute were filled with the smell of burning rubber.

Puberty, pregnancy, the menopause, and hysterectomies seem to be associated with the development of the paragnostic gift in women. In action, paragnosts often pace around like writers seeking the right word. Professor Tenhaeff thinks that there is something in the paragnost which is closer to primitive man or to a young child, an ability to participate in all living things, a lack of a strong sense of self. C. G. Carus, Goethe's friend and doctor, thought the gift was an animal instinct, like the homing power of pigeons. And no one in crowded, urban Holland is prepared to say whether it is something man once had, that has nearly been lost, or something partly there, which it is possible to gain. To an observer it sometimes seems merely an expression of the comprehending closeness that is possible between people, as when Madame de Sevigné said to her daughter (who was suffering from a racking cough), "My dear, I have a pain in your chest."

PART TWO

The
Country
as a
Park

"The Organization of Shortage"

❦ 7 ❦

It is to me one of the most beautiful landscapes in the world. It lies flat under a huge sky, stretched low to a far and flat horizon, against which any interruption, such as a distant town, a line of trees, a church, or a barn roof makes an emphatic silhouette. Trees run along the straight lines of the dikes, banking the canals, or at right angles, Mondrian-fashion, in hedges dividing the canal-drained fields. Seven eighths of what you can see is sky, with clouds filling it, and much of the other eighth is water, reflecting sky, clouds, the leaves of trees and the red-brick of buildings. The rest is green, undershot or overfilled with sand, and in the west, beyond the fields of flowers, banked with dunes which once ran without break all the way from the Hook of Holland to Denmark. The dunes are the natural dike which make the Netherlands possible. This sea-built and wind-formed wall of sand encouraged settlement behind it on stretches of moor and—where the moor had been dug away for peat, for burning—on the islanded clumps of boggy ground that remained. In places mounds of habitation rose amid lakes and marshes; ditches and canals were dug, draining the marshes, connecting the lakes. The well-known saying, attributed to a Frenchman, that God created the world but the Dutch made Holland, perhaps suggests that the Supreme Being would have had the sense to leave this spongy porridge swamp, this homeland of galoshes (as the poet P. H. de Genestet called it) severely alone. But the Dutch settled and persevered. Until this generation they knew as individuals what it meant to dig with a spade, what the power of water was, and how difficult and dirty any sort of reclamation work could be. Nothing in Holland has come without cost. And this cost and difficulty has had its advantages in the orderly Dutch creation, making possible, for one thing, a sharp demarcation between man-made town and man-made country.

Communities grew on piles of earth which were slowly and expensively enlarged to make room for more. Villages spread slowly along widened and heightened sections of dike. To build a house in the western part of the country, where trade and settlement perversely thrived, was to involve oneself in a great deal of communal organization, sand-carrying and pile-driving. In the Middle Ages, severe laws were enforced to help win the battle against water. "No feuds were allowed once the dikes needed repairs," writes Dr. J. van Veen, the historian of Dutch reclamation. Anyone breaking the dike peace by fighting was sentenced to death. "In some parts any man refusing to do his share could be buried alive in the breach with a pole stuck through his body. The people who lived further inland had to come and work at the dike. 'Dike or depart' was the old saying. Any man who was unable to repair the breach in his own section of the dike had to put his spade in the dike and leave it there. This was the sign by which he gave his farm to any man who pulled the spade out of the dike . . . who felt powerful enough to close the breach. This was the *Law of the Spade.*"

Leeuwarden, the capital of the province of Friesland, began as a collection of *terps*—the mounds built as refuges against storm tides and flood. Towns such as Leiden and Middleburg were founded in the eighth and ninth centuries on similar man-made hills, several hundred feet in diameter and fifty feet or so high. Even today, towns like Bergen-op-zoom, which are built on a ridge of dry, sandy soil, are an exception—they have familiar signs of urban sprawl. In most towns and cities, however, haphazard growth has been impossible; the only way to put up a building was to prepare a special site for it. "Every square foot was the result of hard and costly labor and therefore it was necessary to use it with the strictest economy," says the Danish architectural historian, Steen Rasmussen. "The result of all this was limited land and densely built houses rising high into the air rather than spreading out on the ground. In some towns the costliness of the land is literally illustrated by the fact that the tall houses expand towards the top so that the upper stories project far out over the streets." Today municipal and regional authorities can alone bear the huge expense of making the land fit to build on. The recent development of Amsterdam's western dormitory sections, Slotervaart, Slotermeer, Osdorp and Geuzenveld, involved raising the subsoil level by at least six feet. To do this, the Sloterplas polder was excavated over an area roughly a mile long by a quarter of a mile wide, to a depth of ninety feet. The rich polder topsoil was used for parks, lawns, and recreation land, and the twenty-six million cubic yards of sand that were excavated from beneath were used for the preparation of the building sites. The excavation pit was turned into a lake.

In the past, the difficult conditions of construction have not made for drab communities. The English planner Gerald L. Burke has written in a book called *The Making of Dutch Towns*: "The strict regulation of development produced no stereotyped plan, no regimentation, no overbuilding to extract the maximum use from the last square yard." Although houses looked similar, there were often subtle and harmonious differences. Adjacent seventeenth-century houses along an Amsterdam canal "were seldom the work of the same architect, but, although differing in detail as regards façade and gable treatment and window and cornice lines, they usually stood as good neighbours architecturally." Moreover, "one city had a rectangular motif, another a concentric, another a cellular. Yet they were all united by characteristic features, calm, tree-lined canals, some flanked by elegant mansions and others by . . . workshops and warehouses. . . . Above all they shared . . . the dramatic silhouette of tall spires of church, town hall and gate soaring out of the flatness of the landscape, and the pronounced line of demarcation between town and country enforced by the encircling canal." The line still exists. We lived for a month in a house which was, in that particular quadrant of Amsterdam, the very last house in the city. On one side were other houses, a school, gardens, a little street. On the other side, the very edge of town—a six-foot-wide ditch in this case, a rowboat-sized canal, and green, watery fields, lined with similar ditches, and inhabited by ducks, swans, herons, lapwings, and a fourteen-strong-band of black and white cows.

If you are used to the straggle of the American or English metropolitan landscape, what is impressive in Holland is not only this crisp break between town and country but the accessibility of nature and natural things. The core of the Randstad remains agricultural, and water and ducks are everywhere. So a drive of ten minutes from any town of the tight-packed ring of towns will bring you to a place beside a river or canal where you can sit on grass, pick wildflowers, and watch birds—more kinds of birds than you are used to seeing in western, industrial countries. (Starlings, sparrows, and seagulls scavenge our megalopolitan earth.) Meanwhile, grass and flowers are stirring with the wind, which is, like water, a Dutch constant. The elements are earth, fire, water, and air, but in Holland it is moving air. The wind blows without lofty hills to hinder it, brushing over the dunes and across towns and meadows, bringing low clouds and rain from the Atlantic west in all seasons, now and then bearing the summer warmth and freezing winter cold of central Europe from the east, bending trees and turning the few surviving working windmills. The wind drained Holland.

In fine easterly weather one can climb above Holland

in a small plane or, better still, a glider—towed up a
thousand feet from the airstrip at Valkenburg, between
Katwijk and Leiden, and then, catching the right ther-
mals, making use of the wind, lifting in wide arcs until
the country below has become about the size of Madurodam, and not a bit as claustrophobic, banking one way
so that the long white finger of a wing points south toward the Rhine delta, then turning in a lazy circle
which takes in the dunes, polders, lakes, the haze above
the blast furnaces at IJmuiden and the oil refineries at
Europoort, old cities, new developments, all spun together with railroads, motorways, and canals, with pipelines carrying natural gas or sand for building sites.
Soaring thus, you can begin to comprehend this little
country, which on the ground seems so tight and tense, so
complacent and yet so restless, so public-spirited and so
privacy-seeking, busy, booming, and yet for one reason
or another a little more under control than other countries, like a tidy model of the world.

"IF YOU REGARD THE WHOLE OF HOLLAND as one settlement," said Dr. Querido, "it's a house with a garden, and
quite a pleasant one." For centuries there has been competition for space in Holland between town and country,

a competition growing more intense with time, but there
has also been strong rivalry between the separate towns,
with the result that they have all stayed independent
and healthy, and one single city has not dominated the
rest. (Rotterdam and Amsterdam keep up this rivalry
today: if one has an airport, the other must; a subway
system or river tunnel in one city is soon matched by
subway and tunnels in the other.) The two provinces of
North and South Holland were predominantly urban by
the fifteenth century. Johan Huizinga writes: "The economy of our leading region was thus based on a multi-
plicity of small towns crowded together in a small
space and leaving by far the largest portion of the land
covered by water, heath, fields and pastures." With such
a start, the Netherlands is now in the vanguard of a
world on the verge of total urbanization—a fact which
gives some people in the most densely settled country
cause for anxiety. Professor Jac. P. Thijsse, making a
valedictory address to the Institute of Social Studies in
The Hague, in 1966, said: "In 1950 this planet was still
about 20 per cent urban. At present 50 to 60 million people are added every year to the world's total population,
mainly to its urban areas. This rate of growth . . . may
reach 125 million in the year 2000. At that time about 6
billion people may live on earth and two-thirds may be
urban. . . . Thus a tolerable urban development will have
to be built in half a century for 13 times as many people
as in the previous 150 years at a rate 40 times that of the
past. . . . It is of this enormous acceleration that most of
us are not sufficiently aware."

In the struggle for space which urbanization portends, the Dutch in their little room have had some advantages —for one thing, the hard, communal struggle to gain and hold land, giving them a common concern, a common ground, causing them in the words of the British architect, William Holford, "to sink lesser differences and accept a certain discipline in their environment." If planning, as Dr. Querido has neatly put it, is the organization of shortage,* then the Dutch have been planners since the first tribes moved out of the German forests and settled on the coastal heath and marshes. Since 1901, moreover, planning has been understood as encouraging the improvement, by national legislation, of the conditions of city dwellers. The Housing Act of that year merely called for cities with more than 10,000 people to draw up extension plans for adjacent and as yet undeveloped land; but in time these plans—originally no more than street plans—became development schemes for the entire municipal area. Laws were framed to give cities the power to acquire all land involved in a planning scheme and then make various sites available for building purposes.

Today more than two thirds of the land inside Amsterdam limits is owned by the city—a considerable domain (compensating somewhat for the fact that Amsterdam, like other Dutch cities, has very little tax domain, depending for revenue on a proportion of the national

* "The elaborate planning of town and country with its distribution of living, working, shopping and recreation areas, traffic dispositions, green belts, building zones and satellite settlements is nothing but the organization of shortage on a very large scale."

budget set aside in a municipal fund). The city pursues what it calls "an active land policy," acquiring by agreement or condemnation the land it needs, and making ready for building nearly all new building sites. Those prepared by the city, as in the new dormitory developments, aren't sold, but are let out on long, sometimes even perpetual leases—the termination of a lease occurring only when the city wishes to change the use or zoning of the land or alter the form or nature of the buildings (in which case, the leaseholder would be compensated for buildings he had put up). By this means, the city not only keeps a careful, controlling hand on the land, but receives an annual ground rent for its property; this rent is generally adjusted in regard to inflation and changed land values every five years. Rotterdam expropriated much of its land just after it was blitzed by the Germans in May 1940. Thus a harmonious and coherent redevelopment plan could be made for rebuilding it. (The only jarring note is struck by the ponderous office of the Amsterdam-Rotterdam Bank, which institution—according to local legend—stepped in quickly the day after the air-raid and purchased a prime, still-smoldering site.)

Nationally, a Physical Planning Act came into force in 1965, setting up State Planning Commissions, Agencies, and Council in a workable hierarchy, establishing the interdependence of municipal and regional plans, and giving a government minister the right to lay down final, binding regulations. Under this Act there is no formal national plan. But there is a more flexible alternative,

a national physical planning policy, which has been out-
lined (and illustrated with maps) in two reports in 1960
and 1966. "We are not planning for a final thing," said
Mr. J. Vink, former director of the State Physical Planning Agency, "but for a process, and for a never-ending
process at that." The second, 1966 report describes the
various conflicting claims being made on the limited
stock of Dutch land, and attempts to predict a future
pattern of development which will balance these claims.
The report takes into account a heavily motorized nation of 20 million by the year 2000, and creates a "structural scheme" for the country at that time with the hopes
of encouraging "concentrated deconcentration," main-
taining the central open space within the Randstad, and
stimulating the less developed northern, eastern, and
southern areas of the country—which in turn might encourage a more even distribution of people.

In fact, as the geographer Peter Hall points out in
the Randstad chapter of his book, *World Cities*, the population of the west of Holland is expected to sink from
48 per cent to 45 per cent of the total Dutch population
by the year 1981, but because of the natural increase in
the west there will still be a million more people in that
crowded section than there are today. Trends in the
Dutch economy make for further difficulties, particularly
the shift in labor from agriculture and fishing to manu-
facturing and services. The high rate of Dutch national
industrial growth is greatly tied to the Randstad. Oil
refining, the manufacture of petro-chemicals, iron and
steel, and similar "bulky, low-value goods," as Hall calls

them, have transport requirements which cause companies to seek positions on deep, navigable water. The magnetic power of the Randstad is also to be seen in government (whose offices are concentrated there) and in higher education, with most universities now situated in the west. The national planning policy is thus to boost other urban centers outside the west to at least 100,000 people, so that they can really perform and provide the services and attractions of cities. This is being done by such means as inducing firms and factories to go east— Eindhoven and Groningen both offer expanding urban benefits—by opening a new university at Drienloo and attempting to resettle certain government bureaus at Amersfoort. Since, despite all this, the Randstad continues to grow, the policy is to preserve the historic western cities as separate entities with buffers of open space between them, and to preserve the green heart of the Randstad. Here the policy is helped by the fierce demands of the glasshouse farmers and the bulb-field operators; the glasshouse district, hemmed in by Rotterdam, Delft, and The Hague, has actually managed to expand in recent years despite the competition of housing and industry. The expansion of the Randstad will, it is hoped, take place on radial lines, particularly into the Rhine-Maas-Scheldt Delta, and outward to the new reclaimed land in the IJsselmeer.

To a foreign reader, the 1966 planning report seems characteristically (and wisely) Dutch when it stresses the healthy interaction of town and countryside—the latter being no longer just farmland, but the essential

breathing space for people who live in cities. The society considered by the report is dynamic, needing to
communicate, continuously expanding and changing its
ideas, its occupations, functions, and values. The possibility people have of moving greater distances at greater
speed whenever they choose has affected the structure
of society and the demands people make on it. Distance
is less of an obstacle. "Present-day society is character-
ized by the process of scale enlargement, which pene-
trates into all spheres of life," says the report. "It finds
expression in the way some regions are relieved from
their isolation. Mass means of communication and visits
to the town make it possible to copy partly the urban
way of life. The provision of proper transport will result in aspects of urban civilization and social and cultural facilities coming within the reach of the rural
population. However, this often leads to tension between
younger and older generations."

So the country is threatened by the city, and the
Second Physical Planning Report emphasizes the need
to look after the elements of land, air, and water, and to
preserve the distinctions between one sort of environment and another, so that they don't coalesce into a
formless mess. But the Dutch people seem to be aware
of the need for such care and distinctions, and don't
seem to mind (at least in these prosperous times) paying
the cost of the planning process. Part of this may be due
to the shoulder-to-shoulder-together-on-the-dike tradition. One should perhaps also give them credit for con-
sciously taking the public-spirited, long-term view. Sir

William Temple, the seventeenth-century British ambassador, noted the Dutch willingness to be taxed for community projects: "This makes the beauty and the strength of their Towns, the commodiousness of travelling in their Country . . . the pleasantness of their Walks . . . and, in short, the Beauty, Convenience, and sometimes Magnificence, of their Public Works, to which every man pays as willingly, and takes as much pleasure and vanity in them, as those of other Countrys do in the same circumstances among the Possessions of their Families, or private Inheritance." Willem Steigenga, professor of Town Planning at the University of Amsterdam, expresses the same discernment in contemporary terms: "When the community fails to create through its government an environment suitable to provide full scope to society and to human personality, social strain will be the result. . . . An inefficient layout will not only have its impact on the economy but also on human happiness."

Overall Dutch planning seems to have maintained over the centuries a high standard, but there are those who feel that at the level of "layout" or design the Dutch in recent years have not equaled the achievements of their seventy-year-long Golden Age, or even the brief brilliant flashes of the Age of Glass and Concrete earlier in this century. The architectural historian G. E. Kidder Smith, surveying postwar Dutch building, finds many structures which are "outstanding recent Continental horrors." Among Dutch architects the feeling has also been strong that almost everything since the war in Dutch building has been done in the name of speed and quantity, and now has to be the time to seek quality. Several of them, including Aldo van Eyck and Herman Hertzberger, are members of a group called New Ways of Living. In an age of increasing specialization (signaled for me when Bertrand Russell admitted he couldn't understand Wittgenstein), when experts rise in pillars like the topless towers of Ilium, and words like "macrostructure" and "infrastructure" punctuate phrases like "operational research" and "optimal decisions" in every official report, and the reports go unread by people outside a certain field, it has become clear to a few in Holland that the great problem of the age is making sure that the people who have to make decisions possess all the information necessary for a wise decision; that quality will only be obtained by bringing experts together— in the case of New Ways of Living, bringing architects and men like Fiedeldy Dop from other fields to discuss all the aspects of building and living in buildings.

I went one afternoon to visit Ab van Dien, designer and decorator, who is one of the founders of this group, in his experimental house at Heuvelaken, ten miles east of Amsterdam. Van Dien is an athletic-looking man in his late forties with crew-cut grey hair. He told me that he had got together members of Parliament, economists, psychologists, doctors, geographers, sociologists, builders, contractors, industrialists, and a car manufacturer, many of whom attended monthly conferences with a "workgroup" of architects. There are ten thousand registered architects in Holland, a large number for so small a country. Van Dien said, however, that those with individual ideas were few; there were sixteen in the work-group. They were beginning to generate new ideas and projects, and they felt they were doing so at a time of increased public awareness of land-use and design. The Ministry of Housing had made a large grant of two and a half million guilders in 1968 for experimental build-ing, and there were hopes of a tenfold increase in that grant in 1969. The minister himself had opened a confer-ence recently held by van Dien's group at the Amster-dam Municipal Museum. The feeling was becoming more general that the Dutch had to throw off their reputation of being industrious dike-builders and practical car-penters and let a more imaginative vision of man and his life affect the kind of towns they built and the kind of houses they meant to live in. Being Dutch, they were pursuing this imaginative vision as practically as they could.

Van Dien's house was itself an example of what might be done. It was a square, one-story structure, with the living room in the form of a broad cross whose arms ran out to the center of each wall, leaving four rooms in each corner: bedrooms, bathrooms, and kitchen. The house sat very nicely on the ground, well related to the sandy soil and high grass. Chains ran from the roof gutters to the ground, forming a neat conductor for rain water. The materials of the house were plain: a scrubbed pine floor, grey concrete bricks on both inside and outside walls, and a tentlike roof which rose within, with bare cedar beams and exposed reed-and-foam insulation, to a cen-tral skylight. Light also entered from windows on each side set high in the walls, an old device common to seventeenth-century Dutch houses where shutters closed the lower halves of the tall windows and only let in the high, soft light.

There had been a fierce six-month struggle to get permission to build the house. To begin with, said van Dien, they couldn't obtain planning approval, a mortgage, or a contractor. However, the local mayor had been enthusiastic from the start and van Dien got the press interested. The design was published, and people came from all over Holland to see a model of the house. Now it has been built and is connected in a free-form terrace fashion with the nearly identical house of the architect Jan Verhoeven. Verhoeven is also responsible for the design of a series of similar houses the New Ways of Living Foundation is building in Heuvelaken, and an apartment project for retired people in Amersfoort. There, although the three buildings will be ten stories high and communal services will be furnished, the emphasis has been to make each apartment independent and separately flexible, each with its own deliberately private balcony—none of the sidewalks-in-the-sky feeling of the balconies of Osdorp and similar developments.

Some of the impetus of the New Ways of Living group seems to derive from a need to assert individuality in a time of standardization. I suspect that the big, system-built developments are spawning in Holland a school or cadre of radical, individualist architects—an almost poetic reaction against an age of prose. This, too, if you believe that great architecture should tend toward being

anonymous, with no strident signatures, may not be the
ideal answer. However, talking to Herman Klunder, a
tall twenty-nine-year-old champion miler and architect
who practices in a condemned building in Rotterdam
(which he is allowed to use until its demolition), I had
the impression of something quite contrary to intran-
sigent independence. Klunder, the youngest member of
the New Ways of Living architectural work-group, has a
reputation for being an iconoclast and firebrand. He
doesn't subscribe to any architectural magazines, even
the progressive Dutch *Forum*, and has pinned over his
drawing board the sentence EEN FYN GELOOF EEN HYP-
NOTISCHE PUT, which means "A good religion is a
hypnotic trap." But he quotes the Jesuit anthropologist
and archeologist Teilhard de Chardin and admits to an
admiration for Frank Lloyd Wright and Le Corbusier—
and of these two, particularly the latter; Wright (he
says) was not a social architect. Klunder complains that
recent architecture in Holland has not been social
enough. He believes in an architecture that mirrors the
complexity of things and promotes an integrated communal life; in modern Dutch developments all the functions are separate and at any particular time many may
be only partly alive. He thinks the new developments
outside Rotterdam and Amsterdam are horrible, partly
because they are not dense enough. "Their average density is twenty to thirty units per hectare, which is two
and half acres," he says. "Why then does everyone have
this pipedream of living in a house in the old center of
Amsterdam, where the density is two hundred to three

hundred units per hectare?" The new developments are a kind of cellular packaging that fail to promote either privacy or community. Klunder thinks architecture should reflect and encourage the stress between man as a free-wheeling agent in the cosmos and man as a small but necessary contributor to the whole immense natural scheme of things.

Independence and interdependence: the theme was heard earlier in this century in the works and writings of the group known as De Stijl. There, individuality burst forth in reverse proportion to the power with which it was opposed. The members of De Stijl (including Theo van Doesburg, Mondrian, and Gerrit Rietveld) believed in a new consciousness of time, "based on the universal" as they said in their Manifesto of 1917. Art was not to be individual or subjective; it was to be the guide by which man formed and controlled his environment—art perhaps could even be forgotten once man had learned how to direct his environment. And yet nothing could have been less receptive to the variety of the natural universe than De Stijl, with its fierce attachment to straight lines, right angles, and primary colors. When Mondrian took to diagonals there was a crisis and he felt compelled to leave the group. Others broke away more slowly, like the architect J. P. Oud, who later designed such formless, sentimental structures as the Shell headquarters in The Hague. But a few, with Calvinist fervor, stuck to their guns. Gerrit Rietveld, the architect and designer, is perhaps the best example and his furniture is instructive: chairs and stools with every joint visible and every separate part emphasized—by primary paint or elementary carpentry—as a separate part. The result of this, as the British art critic John Berger has pointed out, is extremely expressive furniture opposed to traditional values. (It is also a blunt dismissal of Dutch coziness and bourgeois bad taste.) The Rietveld chair (writes Berger) "proposes that for man to situate himself in the universe, he no longer requires God, or the example of nature, or rituals of class or state, or love of country: he requires precise vertical and horizontal coordinates." He perhaps doesn't require even a chair, for certainly this one is not comfortable to sit in.

The linear, frugal elements of De Stijl are historically Dutch; but now they seem aloof and cold, chilly like the pure white van Doesburg called "the spiritual color of our times." (It is interesting that the contemporary radical group called Provo also adopted white as their color, though with them it seemed to express a humorous and innocent social involvement.) However, here and there in Holland are occasions where De Stijl influence seems beneficent: in the clean, marvelously efficient Dutch telephone booths; in concrete structures such as the sluices at Harderwijk, whose gates are painted in primary colors like the panels of a Rietveld chair; and in several buildings by Rietveld himself, built in surroundings where their Puritan coolness is no disadvantage. I think especially of his pavilion in the sculpture park of the Kroller-Muller Museum, in the Hooge Veluwe woods near Otterloo, Gelderland. There, open on all sides to light and air, an outcrop of steel, glass, wood, brick, and concrete amid the grass and trees, partially sheltering and framing pieces of sculpture by various artists, the principles of the building seem less insistent. The exposed joints and uncapped ends of beams are less dramatized and attention-grabbing. The pavilion is not so much a definitive statement of artistic principle as it is a way of looking, a frame and spectacles through which one sees nature and art and man all interdepending—and, at that, individual rather than universal man, like this girl standing before a piece of carved marble by Barbara Hepworth under the shadow of a grey steel I-beam in the diffused sunlight which falls among the trees.

❦ 9 ❦

NOTHING IS FREE IN HOLLAND, and nothing is wasted. From 1932 to 1968 all the refuse from The Hague was carted daily in special trains to be used as dry compost for improving the sandy soil in Overijssel, 250 kilometers away. Slag from mines is used to make blocks for paving the inner slopes of dikes in the new Delta works, thus helping to clear up mine areas and saving the cost of stone or concrete. A unique music type-face made by Mr. Fleischman of Enschede Printers, in Haarlem, was used in 1766 to print a treatise on how to play the violin, written by Leopold Mozart, Wolfgang Amadeus's father. Although it went unused for the next thirty years, Enschede did not melt it down, and it was found to make an absolutely original, difficult-to-counterfeit border for the paper bank notes they began to print in 1796. Nothing is given away without strings. When Haarlem followed the example of other cities and donated a stained-glass window to the great church at Gouda, it was noticed, on installation, that Haarlem's window showed not only Dutch ships carrying Crusaders up the Nile (where, by the way, the Dutch did considerable reclamation work), but also a beer barrel floating on the Nile waters. This presumably was to whet the thirst of the Gouda congregation for the good beer which was one of Haarlem's biggest exports. (How in fact Haarlem had enough beer to export is a mystery. In 1600 the annual consumption of beer in the taverns of that city was five and a half *million* gallons. The population of Haarlem in 1622 was 39,000, and apparently women drank as much as men. Sir William Temple said, "The qualities in their air may incline them to drinking. . . . It may be necessary to thaw and move the frozen or inactive spirits of the brain.") In butcher shops, the butcher gives you or your children a free slice of liverwurst so that you leave the shop happy and come again. One of the things that has always puzzled and annoyed the Dutch about Rembrandt's tour-de-force, "The Night Watch," is the mysterious little girl-woman who flits among the members of Captain Banning-Cocq's militia company. The militia men all paid to have their portraits in the picture. But what is *she* doing there? How did she get painted for free?

In Holland you pay to go into museums, churches, flower shows, zoos, and toilets. All space is valuable. Even the sky, for sky-writing is still done, and planes tow advertisement banners for various brands of liquorice (to which the Dutch are addicted) above the coastal beaches. In Amsterdam, the chains suspended around major street intersections to control the areas where pedestrians may cross are used for hanging small metal advertisement placards; while you are being prevented from jay-walking you might as well think about buying something. (There are, however, almost no billboards on the roads.) In all but a few Amsterdam cinemas you must leave the theater when the lights go up at the end of the film. If you missed the first twenty minutes and want to see them you have to go out and buy another ticket in order to come in again. To walk in certain sections of the coastal dunes you need a permit, a *wandelvergunning*. It has to be paid for. And, as a Dutchman pointed out to me, what you have to pay for you don't take for granted.

At Katwijk the dunes were a local wilderness and, for us, a salvation. On days when we felt oppressed by the Randstad, by the never-changing view of the sea, and by our landlord, we would walk to the southern end of the Boulevard, past the Sanatorium, past the Camping and the Midget Golf, past the radar station and the wartime German bunkers, beyond the bicycle path that leads to Wassenaar and Scheveningen, and through the turnstile in the high wire fence into the dunes. (There was also a hole under the fence through which we could crawl if the turnstile for some reason was locked.) In the dunes, for a change, the horizon was close and bumpy. The landscape was unfamiliar, natural and ill-kempt: ragged grass, nettles, thorn bushes, scrubby trees. It was a landscape in which everything had a point but a less obvious one than in the level meadows. The dunes are waves, convex on the windward side and slightly concave to leeward. They have been moving and changing for two thousand years or so, driven forward and built up by the wind, shaped and made shapeless, turned into ridges, heaps, and great piles. Sit for a moment on the dune-slope above the beach, and with an onshore breeze you can feel the sand moving. In fifteen minutes you'll be covered with a thin layer of fine-grained sand. But the dunes would move faster if nothing grew on them. Marram grass protects the surface of the dunes against the wind and its roots hold the sandy soil together underneath. Rabbits fertilize the dunes with their droppings (and the herring gulls which nest in and migrate along the dunes hunt the rabbits). Sea spurge, sea holly, lichens, and convolvulus come in the wake of the marram. Thorn bushes, planted on the outside of the existing dunes, catch the sand blown by the wind and cause new dunes to form.

In the Rijksmuseum, there is a small painting by Elias van de Velde (1591–1630): "Duinlandschap." It shows a few people wandering a little forlornly through the same sort of sandy bumps and depression that exist today; a man with a greyhound or whippet; a few rabbits, half-hidden; five birds flying; a scrap of hedge and a wind-swept tree. There is a feeling of it being Sunday afternoon. I prefer the dunes on warm evenings, when you can ramble over the undulating bronze-green hills, looking out for rabbits and trying not to stumble over young Katwijk couples cuddling in the warm hollows. Or in the early morning when you can watch the wilder natural life, the way the eminent Dutch naturalist Niko Tinbergen has done. Tinbergen spent many days watching the gulls at Wassenaar, a few miles from Katwijk. He studied their communities, their territorial habits, and their way of using the updraft over the dunes for less energy-consuming migration along the coast. A gull gets into what Tinbergen calls an "anxiety posture" when a strange gull alights near its territory. It stretches its neck and opens its eyes very wide, apparently deciding whether to fight or to tolerate the intruder. Then it flattens its plumage and keeps its wings ready, in case it needs to take off. Gulls, according to Tinbergen, claim a territory about thirty to fifty yards in diameter, "but in crowded parts of the colony, there are always pairs which select sites rather too close to already settled pairs. This seems to be due to the tendency to nest in a community. In the reproductive instinct, there is an interesting conflict between social traits and the tendency to stake out a territory and defend it against intruders. Both tendencies cannot be fully satisfied because they are antagonistic. Each species of bird has evolved a compromise, ensuring sufficient though not optimal expression for each of the two conflicting tendencies separately, but, as so often in life, the compromise is in itself optimal and has survival value as such."

The dunes are a place where the ingredients of interest are sparse and consequently one's powers of observation are taken up with the few things there: to begin with, birds, insects, and flowers like wallstraw, forget-me-nots, speedwell, fireweed, and ragged robin. On pools and ditches dragonflies hover, and everywhere are ants, bees, and midges. In places the ground is hollow underfoot with rabbit warrens, and just before dark the slopes are alive with rabbits, nibbling and listening, then bounding off at one's approach. Overhead fly lapwing, oystercatchers, chaffinches, and swallows. Each scarp or knoll looks much the same, and it is easy to feel lost, but if you keep going long enough you come over a rise and see the real treasure of the dunes: water, lying in a series of still lakes which are covered with coot and ducks of many kinds, mallard, pintail, shelduck, tufted duck, scoters, and mergansers. Some are swimming, others bobbing up and down while courting; some seem to call to one another and some go whirring off or come splashing down. I sat for a long time one evening watching the ducks on such a lake, listening to their sounds and the sound of frogs croaking and the breeze brushing the sand and the dune vegetation. After a while I became aware of another whirring sound which was somewhat mechanical. I traced it to a concrete-lidded caisson sunk in the ground. From deep within came the sound of a pump pumping water.

At the turn of the century in a cold winter people

skated through the dunes on the chain of frozen lakes
that ran from Katwijk to Scheveningen. By 1935, with
no great change of climate, this was no longer possible.
There wasn't enough water in the ponds. The dunes were
drying up. They were doing so because they formed
the main drinking water reservoir for the west of Holland, and although the Dutch—drinking more beer and
washing less—use much less water than Americans (one
hundred liters a day per capita, compared to five hundred liters a day in the United States); in the Randstad
the Dutch were increasing in numbers and using all they
had. This dune-water shortage had serious side effects.
Rain, falling in the dunes, sifts down through the sand
and hangs in a deep sack underneath, forming a barrier
to the salt water which would otherwise seep in from
the sea and get into the soil of the low-lying land behind
the dunes. (Salt water has a greater specific gravity than
fresh water and thus has to travel beneath it.) As the
salinity of the soil increases, the greater amounts of
chlorine begin to affect plant life: the yield of tomatoes
and tulips declines; so does the milk yield of cows. In
order to preserve then the intensive agriculture of the
Randstad, the Dutch had to preserve the fresh-water
barrier under the dunes. For that matter, since they were
running out of drinking water and the water of the
Rhine and the Maas coming down from Germany and
France was heavily polluted, they had to find a way of
acquiring more fresh water to drink and at the same
time keep the salt out. Salt also enters the country in
locks and rivers, sneaking in along the bottom of deep

channels under fresh water flowing above. Every time the
lock gates at IJmuiden are opened, enough salt comes in
to fill 150 railroad cars; and it is reckoned that there is
already enough salt in Dutch soil to meet world salt
consumption for the next hundred years. The largest
table-salt factory in the world is at Boeklo. Unfortunately
the Dutch haven't yet worked out a way for loading this
salt coming in from the sea in railroad cars, but they
have developed settling basins, just inside the lock gates,
where salt can settle, and also aeration devices, which
keep the salt suspended so that on the next opening of
the gates with a certain sacrifice of fresh water, the salt
can be flushed out to sea again.

Being born with one foot in it, the Dutch perhaps do
not take water for granted quite so much as some other
people. Six out of ten of them live below sea-level. Every
town and province has its waterboard, which is a distinct
and powerful government. At dinner one night in Veere
I overheard four men at a nearby table who talked about
nothing but water throughout their meal. Dutchmen who
have emigrated to Australia have been known to make
arduous journeys just to sit beside a shallow, stagnant
pool. Until well into the nineteenth century cholera,
typhoid, and other waterborne diseases were rife, and
even today more than half of Amsterdam's sewage is
discharged direct into the IJsselmeer. Of course the less
water used, the stronger the sewage, and in warm
weather the smell of town canals is high. In some places
the weather doesn't even have to be warm. You can get a
reminiscent whiff of what the canals in every town used

to smell like in Dokkum, an absolutely beautiful, sleepy
place in Friesland. Along the Westersingel there, roses
have been thoughtfully planted in profusion, but though
they were in bloom when I walked along this canal, they
couldn't wholly camouflage the fact that the Westersingel was a most perfidious ditch. In Amsterdam, summer clouds of black flies and midges settle on your clothing. Driving in the polders, your windscreen is soon
covered with squashed gnats and flying ants. If I lived in
Holland for a continuous, long period I might build up
the proper antibodies, but my present experience is that
every time I come to the country I catch something. As
far as my intestines are concerned, for the first few weeks
of every visit Holland is the Mexico of northern Europe.

You soon understand why the Dutch use two distinct
terms: water is one thing, drinking-water is another.
Most of the surface water in the west of Holland is
either brackish or heavily polluted. A recent poll indicated that the Dutch felt the greatest threat to their
public health came not from traffic or smoking but from
air and water pollution. What particularly affects them
is the river Rhine, several branches of which run through
the country. In 1828 Coleridge traveled in Holland and
Germany and noted:

> *In Köhln, a town of monks and bones*
> *And pavements fang'd with murderous stones,*
> *And rags, and hags, and hideous wenches,*
> *I counted two and seventy stenches,*
> *All well defined, and several stinks!*

The Country as a Park

Ye Nymphs that reign o'er sewers and sinks,
The River Rhine, it is well known,
Doth wash your city of Cologne;
But tell me, Nymphs, what power divine
Shall henceforth wash the River Rhine?

Rotterdam is another city washed by the river Rhine, and people who work there but live elsewhere generally bring a flask of water with them in the mornings to make their coffee or tea. Water taken from the river is kept in open basins for a month and treated with active carbon and a little chlorine, but it is never what one water expert I talked to called "top quality." In spring and summer it is much less than top. Phenols, chemicals, and sewage have left their mark. Rainier seasons help, and so does anything which reduces industrial activity on the upper Rhine and its tributaries, like the French general strike of 1968 or the collapse of Germany in 1945—two occasions when the Dutch noticed a great improvement in the quality of the water. Because the Rhine is an international river, with five countries bordering it, and the Dutch at the lowest, smelliest end (and no divine power has yet shown much interest in cleaning it up), the Dutch have pushed hard for joint action. In 1950 their initiative produced the International Commission for the Protection against Pollution of the river Rhine, which took inventories and made reports. In 1963 the commission was given legal status and a headquarters in Coblentz, and pollution parameter limits were established. The Germans, who cause most of the pollution, have been encouraged to invest 5.5 billion Deutsch marks in sanitation projects. Holland has been putting its own offenders in better order, merging some of its too numerous, autonomous waterboards, building more and better sewage-treatment plants, and forcing some factories to move if they couldn't meet stricter requirements. With the Rhine, some success has been achieved; although more people live and more factories have been built by the river, the pollution has not got worse.

One reason the quality of Rhine water is so important is because the natural dune-water supply now only provides one sixth of what's needed. Since 1955 the dunes providing water to the province of North Holland, to Amsterdam and The Hague and the towns between, have been recharged with water piped from the Rhine. A great part of these dunes is restricted territory. Those, for example, between The Hague and Wassenaar have tracks through them for walkers, cyclists, and horse-riding, and a few sections reserved for naturalists, ornithologists, and the like, who are given entry cards (the number of cards is restricted to 2,000). But the greater part of the dunes is open only to members of the royal family, who go shooting in them once a year (judging by the tameness and profusion of wildlife, they don't hit much), and to waterboard officials. I went in with Mr. S. G. Bos, of The Hague water supply, who told me as we walked along that the bubble of fresh water under the dunes had risen dangerously high by 1955, when infiltration of Rhine water began. The seepage of salt water underneath was by then considerable; it was getting into the drinking water and was affecting the soil and crops of the country behind. But since 1963, the bubble had been going down again, forcing back the salt water as the Rhine water was pumped in. The dunes also act as a stage in the purification of this river water for drinking, though it has been partly treated at the start of its fifty-kilometer journey from the Rhine, and after sinking down through the sand and being pumped up again is further treated in the last stages before being piped out to its 800,000 consumers. In the dunes, this new water has filled old, dried-up natural lakes, and is now filling new man-made lakes. In the last few years the greater wetness of the dunes has changed the environment: some plants have come back which hadn't been seen for a generation—parnassia, a tiny white wildflower, is one—and stinging nettles have arrived, a plant that doesn't belong in the dunes but now seems to flourish in areas wet with river water (which has a lot of artificial nitrogen in it). Reeds are growing in the more nutrient water at the edge of lakes, as are all sorts of algae that wouldn't have thrived in plain rain water. Pike are doing well in the lakes, and so is wildlife in general. Apart from rabbits, several roebuck had come in (Mr. Bos thought they had made the trip from Germany). There were of course gulls, and also pigeons and swans, and on one recently constructed lake we looked at, eleven meters above sea level, with banks on which grass and shrubs were just taking root, the surface of its new water was already covered with ducks. Judging by the way they were swimming, splashing, and ducking, doing everything ducks generally do, it had their approval.

❦ 10 ❦

THE DUTCH HAVE A RIGHTFUL PRIDE in their long struggle for land and space. It is the patriotism of people who know they are responsible for the creation and preservation of their *patrie*. Since the year 1200, roughly 1,700,000 acres have been gained and 1,400,000 acres lost. Very few Dutch families lack a book or two on land-reclamation works, and many can bring forth a set of annual reports, issued between the two great wars, describing the construction of the dam—the *Afsluitdijk*—which closed the Zuider Zee, turned it into a fresh-water lake renamed the IJsselmeer, and made possible the empoldering of part of its waters. In the spring of 1968 many made their own informal pilgrimages to see the first new land appear from the draining of the third of the four planned polders. For fifty years nearly 2 per cent of the national income has been spent on dredging, draining, and reclaiming, and the Dutch find romance in engineering figures and in calculations of subsidence, salinity, or tidal flow. At Delft there is another miniature world which does a lot in my mind to balance Madurodam—a hydraulics laboratory where the models are not houses and castles but riverbeds, dikes, harbor entrances, and sluices in enclosure dams. Swell generators create the effects of sea; wind flumes make waves, even gale-driven waves; and small, spinning cylinders, which cause water particles to move, reproduce the effect (known as the Coriolis effect) that the daily rotation of the earth has on the flow of water in oceans, lakes, and wide rivers. The entry of salt water is studied in an ingenious device which allows two different sorts of water to flow in one model. Studies at Delft have been done for British Columbia and Belgium, for Nigerian harbors and works in the Persian Gulf. But in recent years the big task of the laboratory has been model-making for the complicated system of dams, sluices, storm barrages and strengthened dikes which are being built on the vulnerable coastline of the Rhine-Maas-Scheldt Delta region. In 1840 the salt coastline of Holland was 1,230 miles. It is 840 miles now. But when the Delta plan is finished in 1980 it will be reduced to some 420 miles.

Today, although most Dutchmen no longer know what it is as individuals to shovel sand into a breached dike, they remain aware of the proximity of water and its power. "The currents are dangerous," people told us as we prepared to swim off the beach at Katwijk. "The IJsselmeer is dangerous," we were told when it was known that we were sailing across it from Lemmer to Enkhuizen. "The Waddenzee is dangerous," we heard at Oostmahoorn. At Katwijk in the early morning cars and *brommers* draw up for a moment on the way to work so that their drivers and riders can take a thoughtful look at the sea—partly perhaps because it is a pleasant thing to do and also perhaps because of a need to make sure the sea is still in its proper place. Eight million out of twelve and a half million Dutchmen cannot swim. And although we believed we could handle the Katwijk currents, safely navigate the IJsselmeer, and get from Oostmahoorn to Schiermonnikoog without calling out the lifeboat, we didn't scoff. The Dutch respect for their ancient adversary is sound. You have only to stand on the seafront of one of those coastal towns on a winter or even an equinoctial night when an onshore gale is blowing, and sand and spray are flying inland, to find a little color in hitherto listless facts: 2,300 pumping stations, 1,200 miles of dune and dike, and the land itself sinking at roughly one millimeter a year.

In winter, watch is kept along the dikes and twice-daily weather forecasts announce any expected differences of high-water level. On January 31, 1953, orange flags were flying all over Holland in honor of the fifteenth birthday of Princess Beatrix: those flags streamed out in an increasingly stiff breeze. At 6 p.m. the pilot boats stopped leaving port. There were reports of many ships in distress in the North Sea. At 11 p.m. the roaring of the wind probably ensured that more people than usual were still awake to hear from the radio: "During the night and tomorrow morning severe northwesterly gales ... unsettled weather with variable cloud and scattered showers, hail and snow." Unsettled was the word. It was *onrustig* weather. The gales accompanied spring tides, the highest tides. The northwest wind drove a mass of water down the North Sea into the funnel between southern England and the Low Countries. In the Delta region between Rotterdam and Antwerp the alarm bells rang and in towns and villages men mustered as the sea rose higher than it ever had before, in some protected spots simply washing over the dikes while in others it smashed through them with great blows. On the island of Flakkee fourteen continuous miles of dike went down. On another stretch four miles of railroad track washed off the top of a dike thirty-four feet above mean sea level. Altogether six hundred gaps were made in the dikes and nearly eight hundred miles of dike were destroyed. At Colijnsplaat in the Delta a band of men put their shoulders to a wall of sandbags in a breach and held it until the water went down, thus saving their village from inundation. At Ouderkerk on the branch of the Rhine called the Hollandsche IJssel, a skipper ran his old barge into the bank where he saw a breach actually being formed. It was a night and a following day of many heroes, but even so a fathom of swirling water covered more than 400,000 acres of land, flooding farms and villages. Some 1,795 people lost their lives, tens of thousands of animals drowned, 2,500 buildings were completely destroyed and 15,000 seriously damaged, and of course machinery, crops, and fodder were lost. Nor was the damage just immediate. Tidal currents continued to scour deeper and less repairable holes in the dikes, and further gullies formed far inland with every tide. Fields were covered with layers of sea-sand, and the soil was given lethal soakings of salt.

On the following days people drove from the Randstad and pitched in to the work of rescue and repair. A million guilders was collected in a national appeal. Aid came from other countries, and 6 per cent of that year's Dutch budget went to restore the damage. Seventeen million sandbags were needed, 133 tugboats, 8 Second World War 7,500-ton concrete caissons and 696 smaller caissons. In one gap alone, at Ouderkerk, (where 40 million cubic meters of water rushed through at each flood-tide, two thousand men worked until November 6 before closing the gap. Before the first anniversary of the storm all the flood water had been pushed out again, but it was seven years before Dutch agricultural production fully recovered from the devastation.

❧

I spent a week wandering in Zeeland, the province most smitten by that flood. The motto of Zeeland is *Luctor et emergo* ("I struggle and emerge") and its emergence continues, not only from the dangerous grip of the sea with the aid of the expensive, complicated Delta plan, but from the past. Old and new are posed dramatically: farmers drive their cars to Middelburg market to look at huge roan shire horses, tails and manes plaited with ribbons, ridden by lads wearing black wide-awake hats. On the side of the modern highway to Goes an old dame totters along in white clogs, wearing black shirt and stockings, blue apron, a shawl crossed over the front and fastened at the back, and a stiff white-lace bonnet, tight on her head, with gold filigree bobbles like curlers stuck along the hairline at the front. At Yerseke there are still medieval oyster sheds, but also billboards advertising vacation bungalows and camping sites near the Yachthaven—the oysters will go and the summer people will come in the course of the next ten years as the East Scheldt is dammed. Dams and dikes bring construction machines, material, men, and money into the backwater of Zeeland. Roads are built, and bridges connect islands. Distances shorten, scale enlarges, and industry finds new room, land, and labor at better prices. Zierikzee, for instance, is an old market town you enter through a slightly cockeyed medieval gateway and drive around a lady beating an oriental rug in the middle of the main street. There people say they are annoyed by these intrusions, but the banks of course have the international rates of exchange posted in their windows and the Hotel Concordia flies the flags of twelve nations.

I had lunch at the Concordia with Mr. K. J. M. Gerritzen of the Ministry of Transport and Waterways. Mr. Gerritzen had pea soup and ham and eggs while I had a Concordia omelete. (The *Guide Michelin* 1967 lists no three-star restaurants in the Netherlands. There may or may not be any pianos in Japan, but I can say, with deep conviction, there are no omelettes in Holland.) Mr. Gerritzen, a trim, genial man in his mid-forties, told me about the Delta plan, whose only large drawback he believed to be the loss of the oyster and mussel beds in the eastern Scheldt. Otherwise in this region which looks from above like a spread-out farmer's hand—the thick fingers being islands and peninsulas—most of the openings will be blocked, shortening the coastline. The western Scheldt will remain open, giving access to Antwerp, and so will the New Waterway which leads to Rotterdam, with its dikes raised and strengthened, and a storm-flood defense gate built on the Hollandsche IJssel five miles inland from the city. The new system of dams and sluices will divert the so-called fresh water of the Rhine down the New Waterway, helping to push back the incoming salt water, and will provide fresh water for the irrigation of the Zeeland fields. Most of all, calculations of North Sea tide and weather over a hundred years show that the Delta plan will reduce the chances of flood disaster to roughly one in ten thousand. The cost of these improvements and security will be about three thousand million guilders or nearly one thousand million dollars, spread over twenty years. Comparable to the cost of the Tennessee Valley Authority dams and lakes, it will form about 1½ per cent annually of the Dutch national budget. However, the Dutch in their thrifty way have worked it out that there is a direct return in savings and profit of half that amount, so the actual cost of the plan is only three quarters of 1 per cent of the annual bill for running the nation.

After lunch I drove to Haringvliet with Mr. Gerritzen. Haringvliet is one of the major estuaries in the Delta, allowing the escape of more than half the Rhine-Maas flow, and when it is dammed, and this flow has been diverted down the New Waterway, there will have to be means to get rid of overflow at this point. In the mouth of the Haringvliet, therefore, a set of giant sluices is being built in the dam, capable of letting through not just water but great quantities of drift ice (which will form faster when the water behind the dam is less salt and not moving). The dam carries a roadway, part of the new Rotterdam-Vlissingen highway joining the Delta islands. In the dam is incorporated a shipping lock, and a fishing harbor for the boats from the villages of Goedereede and Stellendam, which will soon be less accessible from the sea.

It was a fine, breezy day. We drove out over the lock, past the fishing harbor, and across a ramshackle prefabricated bridge which, since the dam was not yet complete, spanned the gap to the sluices in the middle of the estuary. The sluices had to be built first so that they could be opened and allow water to move in and out while the rest of the estuary mouth was being blocked. "We put the sluices here because to build them we had to make an artificial island with a lake in it, in fact a diked pit, and here the water was fairly shallow," said Mr. Gerritzen, holding onto his hat. "At Delft they first made models of the island and the estuary. Then in 1957 the work here began—first a service harbor was built on the north shore of the Haringvliet, then a ring dike was made out here in the middle by dumping clay and then pumping sand behind it, and then closing the final gap with stone, gravel, and twenty caissons. Dredgers inside the pit excavated it to the right depth for the sluices—we remembered to leave a gap for them to float out. Then the gap was closed and the water pumped out. One consequence of putting the pit on the shallows in mid-estuary was that the deep-water channel was scoured out from a depth of thirty-six feet to sixty-six feet—the Haringvliet made up in depth what it lost in width. A pumping station was built inside the pit, not only to keep the floor of the pit dry but to dry out strata deep beneath it. We didn't want several underground springs to well up suddenly. Preparation for the above-surface building involved the driving of sheet-steel pile walls, 24,000 tons of it, and then to support the bays and piers of the sluices, 21,842 precast concrete piles were hammered in. After the sluices were built and the steel gates fitted, we dredged away the encircling dike. It cost twenty million guilders to build and ten million to remove."

The sluices are huge. From the unfinished four-lane roadway running along the top of them, fifty feet above the waters of the Haringvliet swirling through the open gates, I had the disconnected feeling one might have halfway up a pyramid or alone in an empty Olympic stadium; the sort of feeling which makes one say, "This would be a good set for a Hitchcock thriller." However, Mr. Gerritzen happily brought forth details which tended to bring the gargantuan into scale, such as a bicycle track alongside the four motor-traffic lanes, and fish culverts in every other pier. There were inflatable rubber seals between the steel gates and the concrete of the piers to reduce seepage (especially valuable because the steel gates expand and shrink with changes of temperature). Electric heaters in the seals prevented the rubber from cracking in freezing weather. Iron rams on the inshore side of the piers helped break up large floes of ice. Inner and outer gates could be partly opened to let a little salt water in to help melt the ice. On the inland side there was a deep sill just in front of the sluices for salt to settle in. The concrete girders which form the framework of the sluices were assembled on the spot, in the working pit, from six-foot-thick equilateral pie-shaped concrete sections, strung together point-downward on more than a thousand steel cables. Wet concrete was put like glue between these precast wedges, and then they were winched together, the stress transmitted by the cables changing them from a mere assembly of separate segments into a single immensely strong structural member weighing 8,700 tons. Between the piers under the girder there are seventeen gates on each side. Each gate has a 185-foot-long blade, like a giant snow plough, which swivels up and down on long steel arms, worked by hydraulic pistons powered in turn by surprisingly small electric motors. At this time the sluice building was running a little behind schedule because minute cracks had been discovered in some of the gate hinges, and the hinges had to be returned for repair ("to Belgium," Mr. Gerritzen noted dryly). A tower at one end of the sluices controls the gates with the aid of electronic processing equipment which analyzes information about water levels, discharge rates, wind force, wind direction, wave height, and salt content. The width and substance of each gate has been determined by the power of ice and the pressure of the sea. "We don't think we have forgotten anything," said Mr. Gerritzen.

Migrating birds are already following the new coastal route of dams and dikes, connecting the seaward sides of the Zeeland islands. Moreover, dunes are beginning to form in front of some of the dikes as the sea, unable to get into its old channels, throws up sandbanks. The resulting dunes will protect the dikes and indeed in some places make them unnecessary, though without them the dunes wouldn't form.

Was it Montaigne who said that children play at what they will work at as men? On the Boulevard at Katwijk small boys with toy trucks cart away the sand their sisters sweep up with child-sized brooms, while on the beach below, babies sit, pawing the sand between their legs and then lifting and letting fall infant fistfuls of damp grains. One remembers that the Dutch in previous centuries have drained the English fens and the Russian marshes—and perhaps, if they ever get Holland squared away, they can be commissioned to drain a needy area like the Ganges Delta, too. But Holland still calls, and to see more of a traditional dike under construction, somewhat less of an engineering spectacular than the Haringvliet sluices, I went a little farther south with Mr. Gerritzen one morning to see the barrier being built across the Brouwershavengat, between the islands of Goeree and Schouwen-Duiveland. This dam-works was also an island just then, to be reached only by boat. We sailed in a steel diesel launch, run by a man wearing a blue turtle-neck sweater—a seaman whose weathered, wrinkled features indicated no nationality but rather that he hailed from any North Sea port. He might have been from Malmö or Esborg, Bergen or Nordeich, Flamborough or Hull. (I am told that the fishermen of Friesland can understand the fishermen of Yorkshire better than they understand a burgher from Amsterdam.)

We walked along the new dike, on which dandelions and grass had already established themselves, while a lark flew overhead. The launch went back to the work harbor to collect a party of schoolchildren, come to get acquainted with the long Dutch struggle and to see how they were winning it. Mr. Gerritzen pointed out as we strolled along where the highway would be, and the nature refuge and yacht harbor, in which ducks were presently cruising. He told me how many million cubic meters of water were involved, and how many thousand tons of rock and clay. Here in the Brouwershavengat an aerial cableway was being used to dump boulders in the channel between the islands and the dam so far completed. Unlike rock-carrying barges, the cableway could work in the roughest weather. He pointed out the place where the caissons would be pushed in by tugs at the dramatic moment, when the tides were still, to close the final gap. The caissons would then be built into the finished dike. We walked down the shallow face of it on the seaward side—it was in fact a stone and asphalt-faced slope with first a gentle and then a steeper escarpment, designed to take the punch out of the waves. Mr. Gerritzen said that both angles were shallower than those used in the design of the Afsluitdijk in 1932. There were improvements, too, in the construction. Formerly, brushwood mattresses weighted with stones protected the face of dikes and the channelbeds where caissons were to rest. But the amount of brushwood available in the Biesbos area of the Delta had become insufficient for all the dike works and was, moreover, liable to attack by teredo worm. So nylon mattresses have been developed, with pockets that can be filled with sand or stone to ballast them. Machines have been devised to coat these mattresses while under water with a layer of asphalt. Stones to face the undersea slopes of the dike can then be lowered and placed neatly in plastic-covered wire baskets—an Italian idea, used in the Po Valley. I wasn't surprised to learn that the Dutch were using radar to study the behavior of waves, and radioactive isotopes to follow the movement of sand under the sea. And though in the channel coming to the dike there had been a stern chop, it seemed to me that these grey North Sea waves rolling up to the dike in the Brouwershavengat quickly put on their best behavior.

❧

Water and sky conspire to make Zeeland one of the most spacious of Dutch provinces. The horizon is never-ending. In Zeeland there is, as well, something like an expansive gesture, and an expensive one, taken at the cost of 70 million guilders by the Provincial Waterboard. This authority decided not to wait until 1980 for the completion of the dam and roadway across the East Scheldt to open up the southern islands to contemporary development, but to build its own three-mile-long bridge, with twin roadways, a bicycle track, lane-dividing barriers, and a low guard-rail over which the motorist has a splendid view. It is at once a sweeping yet controlled statement, expressed in long, prestressed concrete arcs which rest on concrete biped structures, seeming from above to lie across the water like a straight and simple chain, and from water level to run in the continuing rhythm of the dikes. It presents no jolts to the eye. It flows.

Over the Zeeland bridge, having paid a toll of three guilders, one can drive to Noord Beveland, Walcheren, and Veere. For if the Zeeland bridge harmonizes man's engineering ability, his desire to be mobile, and his environment in a way that lets one know that the twentieth century can produce not only compromises between technology and human ecology but their mutual triumphs, then Veere demonstrates that Holland has had previous achievements in those respects. Like Dokkum, Kampen, Hoorn, Elburg, and Zutphen, Veere is an architectural declaration of vigilance, care, and past prosperity. Ringed by a dike, it is half a dozen streets crowded with old brick houses and a harbor whose waters are now fresh and tideless (the Veersegat, one of the earliest Delta works, was dammed in 1961), and whose vessels are now yachts rather than fishing boats. Veere was perhaps never a good example of the fact, evident in larger towns, that for the great majority the Golden Age had little glitter: it was long miserable hours of work, hovels to live in, and plague and other diseases to take one to an early grave. The urban problems of the sixteenth and seventeenth centuries were probably always less in smaller towns, say, than in Leiden, with its textile mills.

In Veere, where sugar was unloaded from the Canaries for the first time in 1508, rich cargoes made rich captains and merchants, and today it is the golden past almost unalloyed. The Raadhuis, formerly the wool mart and begun in 1474, has a steep roof bolstered by two corner battlements, dotted with numerous tall dormer windows, and topped by one of those high, fanciful towers, rising in galleries, belfries, arcades, and bulbous steeples, into which all the romance and imagination of old Holland seems to have been flung—the signature of a town visible from afar against the sky. I was in Veere on the Queen's birthday, when the southwest wind was shaking the orange flags, banners, and wimples that were flying everywhere. At dawn, a bugle sounded from the tower of the church. That morning, when I looked in, it was as if soldiers of the Reformation had been there not long before, for most of the huge barnlike structure is an empty shell, with a dirt floor and wooden-pole scaffolding that seems to hold it up, and is used as a shed for storing old carriages and the *brommers* of the choir. But everywhere else in Veere present prosperity has made things right. In the evening, the wind had died, the weathervanes were still, and the sunlight on the old bricks had enough warmth in it to dry out all the damp in Holland. Looking at one small street, I saw that instead of a curb, bricks were laid in a certain pattern to

mark the border between sidewalk and street, and had
different strengths of color to distinguish the sidewalk
from the border of a house—the purpose of a particular
piece of space being indicated by nothing more than
shade and pattern.

❦ 11 ❦

SOMETHING OF THE SAME NATURAL SKILL in the ordering
of an environment is evident in the new harbor section
of Rotterdam called Europoort. The scale is much larger,
the resources are greatly different, and much has inevi-
tably disappeared from the intimate relation of things.
Going from Veere to Europoort is a leap from time past
to time future, and the two names give some indication
of the difference, Veere with its soft, localized two syl-
lables, and Europoort with its promotional suggestions of
international trade. Yet it is the prosperity that Rotterdam generates which keeps Veere looking so pretty.
Rotterdam is now the largest and busiest port in the
world, having surpassed New York in 1963. Everything
is the biggest there: the world's tallest chimney (650
feet), the world's largest drilling rig, the highest capacity
grain terminal in Europe, the world's largest container
loading and unloading operation. The superlatives have
a New World ring about them, but Rotterdam makes one
wonder if the New World in many ways isn't getting

rather old. The city has had the advantage of a late start. Holland came after most other European countries into the Industrial Revolution. Its rivers and harbors had badly silted up, and Dutch ships were forced to be of such shallow draft they couldn't compete with the deeper, more commodious ships of England and France. Machinery—especially mechanical dredges—rescued it from economic ruin in the early nineteenth century, and in Rotterdam, whose New Waterway was dug out by those first steam dredges, one now has the impression that machinery and automation give the Dutch the ability to go on digging and building and extending forever: after Rotterdam, Botlek; after Botlek, Europoort; after Europoort, Maasvlakte, pushing out from the present line of the coast into the North Sea—and then, glancing at the development maps, one sees that Maasvlakte takes a bend to the south and extends down, outside the Voorne dunes, and shadows the beach and woods of the village of Rockanje. The fact that right now Maasvlakte is underwater, offshore, means little. The Rotterdammers have the means and the enthusiasm to turn it into cargo loading areas, warehouse facilities, deep channels, refineries, roads, tunnels, and docks for bigger and bigger ships, with little more difficulty than the Katwijk children making harbors in the sand. "For a while we thought the limit was a ship of 65,000 tons," said Ivo Blom, a large and friendly thirty-five-year-old Rotterdam official, as we drove out to Europoort. "Then we thought 100,000 tons. Now we are working on a seven-mile-long channel seventy-two feet deep, giving a 240,000-ton tanker 20 per cent clearance at lowest spring tides. But we can dredge down to one hundred feet. We will be able to take care of 500,000-ton tankers. Our only limit is the depth of the North Sea."

In Rotterdam harbor the water even in calm weather is a white-capped jumble of wakes and bow-waves from the mass of moving craft. Annually, 250,000 barges pass through the harbor, many of them being oil lighters heading for the refineries at Europoort. There, the big round storage tanks extend mile after mile. ("If every person in Holland brought eight liters of oil, it would just fill one tank," said Mr. Blom, in as offhand a way as he could manage with so burdensome a fact.) Weird conglomerations of vats, tanks, scaffolds, tubes, and pressure domes stand in uninhabited compounds, and strangely elegant chimneys let off stinks and flares. Here and there are structures which look like offices or control buildings, but no one seems to be going in or out of them, or leaning out of the windows. It is perhaps the world where machines operate machines. "Over there," said Mr. Blom, waving at a scrubby oasis as we cruised by, "is a recreational area." He didn't sound as if he expected it to be there long. "And that building is the new seamen's hostel. We're too far out for the men to be able to get into town. There used to be a bird sanctuary where the BP refinery is now—I used to come out here from school on nature trips. We're already handling 76 million tons of crude oil a year, and we'll have a refining capacity of 60 million tons plus in 1970. That over there is a States Mines subsidiary; they use enough electricity for a city of 350,000 people. There's ICI, integrated plastics. Fertilizer here. Carbon there. We serve the whole middle west of Europe. Have you seen those old cranes they use to unload the ships in London—ships lying tilted over on the mud at low tide? We will handle a hundred thousand containers this year. It is an explosion in cargo-handling techniques, and we are ahead in it. Big ships come in here and transfer their containers to little ships for England and Scandinavia."

We got out of the car at the end of a newly paved road, where there was a small knoll, a pile of bulldozed ground, from which we had a view out over the newly reclaimed flats where new havens were being dug. There were still no people. I took comfort in the sight of a field mouse that darted across the road. In the main channel of the New Waterway we could see a giant tanker coming in. There was very little suggestion of motion, and yet it moved. It seemed blind, and yet it didn't seem to need the tugs that scurried alongside its smoothly gliding bulk. "There are seven radar towers along the Waterway," murmured Mr. Blom. "Ships can come in safely in all weather. These tankers have very small crews, for everything is automated. It takes them only twelve hours to unload and turn round. My brother-in-law used to sail on one. He couldn't stand it."

❦

Oil for the Ruhr and Holland. Oil to heat the houses, run the factories, and move the cars of Europe. A hundred years ago, one and a half lifetimes, the fuel in

Holland was peat. The peat was dug by hand in the moors and loaded by hand into forty-ton sailing barges which a man—with the help of his wife and a boy— could sail through Holland, selling his cargo to farmers and householders. Today a barge below one hundred tons is uneconomical, and barge skippers are given government grants if they allow their vessels to go to the ship-breakers. Oil or natural gas comes in a pipe and is metered as it is used in the house—and in most places, particularly in the west of Holland, that house is not the result of one man deciding that's what he wanted for a home; it is the result of decisions by planners, architects, engineers, politicians, housing associations, and committees. Proper names are replaced by initials and abbreviations, as if they would simplify a complexity too great for us. And a three-hundred-thousand-ton tanker is no longer a ship, even an immense ship. It is the sum of a thousand technological possibilities, some of which we aren't sure we have even begun to grasp. Is this what we really wanted? Did we build this just because it could be built?

Rotterdam encourages such speculation on the kind of world man is actively and perhaps not too thoughtfully creating. It is in many ways a brand-new city. It is bustling, on the make, paying more taxes to the nation than any other city as a result of its big companies and imports. It has its Eurotower, an up-to-date observation tower in concrete, and a shiny, quiet single-line subway. It is working on a World Trade Center. The city crystalizes in concrete, glass, and steel the phoenix feeling which every Dutchman inherits—the feeling of making things from scratch, starting from ashes: in this case the result of the German air raid of May 14, 1940. What has been built in the center has been widely praised, particularly the Lijnbaan shopping precinct, with its pedestrian malls, sidewalk cafés, and adjacent hotels, apartments, concert hall, and underground parking garage. In style, the Lijnbaan has two apparent sources—one close by, in the Van Nelle biscuit factory built in 1928 and still modern though in the same cold airport control-tower pattern; and the other, at a distance, in the American postwar store architecture of Morris Ketchum. Yet, for all the pleasantness of its scale, and the pleasure one feels at being able to walk around it, the Lijnbaan seems drab and machine-made. The surrounding streets seem too wide for the height of the buildings placed along them; the width emphasizes such distracting features as overhead tram wires and the posts supporting them. (One of the Dutch architectural reactions to "overcrowding" has been this expansiveness where space and few traditional restrictions exist. This can also be seen in the Amsterdam dormitory towns; in the southeast Flevoland capital of Lelystad; and in Nagele, one of the new villages of the northeast polder, where the rows of houses are set so far from each other that they scarcely form a community.) The Dutch themselves think Rotterdam is a cold town, and certainly on grey days concrete and glass are not the most cheerful materials. However, time helps. In the dormitory section of Pendrecht, where the blocks of apartments are not altogether well liked by their inhabitants, there are also single-family houses and low blocks

CEES VAN DER MEULEN

North Sea waves.

Walcheren: modern dike.

CAREL BLAZER

Amsterdam, the center city.

In the Begijnhof.

Apartments in Buitenveldert.

Worker in a Drachten factory.

Wortman Pumping Station: the modern windmill.

Bicycles and brommers.

The Amstel in Amsterdam.

Europoort—new harbors.

Ab van Dien's experimental house, designed by Jan Verhoeven.

J. VERHOEVEN

Interior of van Dien house.

J. VERHOEVEN

Wadloping.

Cyclists on a dike.

of old people's flats amid the larger towers; trees are
growing, and the whole place seems, as one walks around
it, to be well used.

Perhaps because their town is cold and new, Rotterdammers themselves are friendly (in historic, charming,
and cozy Amsterdam, the natives are more sophisticated
and less hospitable). But one soon notices that the places
to which the friendly Rotterdammer invites a guest are
not a spacious new Lijnbaan restaurant or his modern
apartment, but some small hole-in-the-wall bar in a
crumbling nineteenth-century house. There are still a
number of such houses in Rotterdam, most often condemned, and many are lent by the city to artists and
architects to use as studios until the time comes to pull
them down. In others, in tenements on the Witte de
Withstraat, for instance, there are shabby refuges, pubs
for newspapermen and writers and sculptors and designers—all of whom, cheerfully drinking their beer and
genever, have congregated in Rotterdam because it
excites them and pays them, enabling them to work and
then to take cover in one of the bars where the friendly
noise is so great they can't hear the machine they have
helped to make—this great oil-dispensing, grain-
handling, chemical-creating, apartment-building machine,
working its way down the street, gobbling up old buildings.

Intimations of the New Babylon, the new Leviathan.
Jammed in at Mr. Pardoel's, a pub in the Binneweg.
Thick with beer smell and tobacco smoke. Mr. Pardoel,
says Ivo, is a millionaire who runs the bar for fun. That's

Mr. Pardoel, the little man behind the counter giving you the change from a two and a half guilder note. Always closes at eight—yes, EIGHT P.M. The clock doesn't work. He'll tell you when to clear out. The old man by the door is a drunken fossil who once worked for Rietveld, the great designer, and is respected. The sculptor in the corner with the gorgeous girl brings in a new gorgeous girl every week. Sculptors and artists are mostly on annual grants from the city, which, like other cities in Holland, sets aside 1 per cent of all building costs for art works and landscaping. That man next to the bar is a maker of documentary movies, a type of film-making for which men like Haanstra and Joris Ivens have gained Holland a great reputation. There are conversations about the police, who are out of touch; about someone's mother, who is too much in touch; about somebody's dirty film and how the man who made it lost so much money he is now living in his own attic and renting out rooms in the rest of the house; and about the Rotterdam soccer team and its chances of beating Ajax, of Amsterdam. The Rotterdam face is a working face, with strong nose and cheeks, dark hair. . . . Mr. Pardoel's pub is being pulled down next year.

However, progress is not quite running rampant. There is a growing official awareness in Rotterdam that what counts now is not the design of projects, like the Lijnbaan or Pendrecht, but the design of a region; that the glass-house districts of the Westland and the open spaces of Voorne, south of Europoort, and the industrial development of smaller Delta towns like Oosterhout, are crucial

items in a single juggling act. Rotterdam and its region
are presently working to control air-pollution. An eighty-
meter mast for continuous measuring of pollution has
been set up at Vlaardingen, in the center of the region,
and a central supramunicipal authority called Rijnmond
has been established, with an environmental health
commission which has the power to investigate complaints and try to remedy the offending physical or
chemical processes at the source.

Even so, when the wind is in the southeast, as it fortunately isn't too often, The Hague is highly aware of
Rotterdam, and government officials wonder whether it
isn't so powerful a weight the whole country will swing
with it. One staff member of the National Physical
Planning Agency pondered aloud about Dutch money-
making characteristics, and whether Rotterdam might
not be expanding simply for expansion's sake. "We have
a good reputation for looking after our land," this official
said, "but I'm not sure whether on this scale we have
made all the correct calculations—whether, in fact, a
new oil refinery at this point brings in money to the
country or costs the country more than it makes. The
deeper the channel of the New Waterway, the more salt
that enters. The more salt that enters, the more danger
to the drinking water of Rotterdam and to the soil of the
Westland agriculture land, and the more Rhine water
needed to expel it. If you look at the development-
possibilities map of the Rotterdam-Europoort-Delta region, you'll see an anchorage area for mammoth tankers
off the Hook of Holland. There we have then the possi-

bility of offshore unloading. We have the possibility of more tankers—and the more risk of oil spillage. Even now the North Sea beaches from Scheveningen to Den Helder are often pockmarked with tar."

Our landlord in Katwijk kept a bottle of gasoline inside the front porch, with a rag for applying it to the soles of our shoes when we came in from a walk along the beach, and he went into furious sulks if some tar escaped this treatment and got trodden onto his stair carpet.

❦ 12 ❦

WHEN SPACE SEEMS IN PARTICULARLY SHORT SUPPLY, as it does on the beach at Katwijk on any Sunday, and one feels the need of exterior rather than interior space, one should fight one's way out on the packed Randstad roads eastward to the woods of the Veluwe, or northeastward to the IJsselmeer polders, the reclaimed land of the Zuider Zee. The Dutch call it "the new land." In 1932, when Cornelius Lely's plan reached its first stage of success with the completion of the enclosing dike across the mouth of the Zuider Zee, it was taken for granted that the ground slowly reclaimed from the lake would be used for agriculture: for crops needed for home use or export; for farmers who needed larger, more efficient farms, and for farmer's sons who wanted to be farmers in their turn. And in two of the four big polders, the northeast polder and the East Flevoland polder, this has been the case—farming is the thing—although in East Flevoland there are hints of a change: there are fewer villages, an extra town. People no longer want to live in small hamlets. Cars and motorcycles make it possible for them to get to work from larger places which provide more services and a greater variety of shops, people, and attractions. With the Common Market, many crops are available more cheaply from Italy or France; agriculture has also lost its priority status, and every year less Dutchmen are engaged in farming. In time, moreover, the new polders have been recognized for their national value, not just for a local, agricultural value. The new polders allow for new road routes, new railways, and room for the expansion of Amsterdam. So in the southern Flevoland polder, which has just been drained, less than half the new land will be used for farms. A quarter of it will provide space for a new town, a satellite of Amsterdam, and space for industry. Another quarter will be space for the constricted to stretch their elbows—there will be beaches on the border lakes between old land and new, and woods, with trails and bridle paths, on land that in any case might be too sandy for crops. Planning has become social—and man, man is becoming leisured: the *homo ludens* of Johan Huizinga's prophetically entitled book.

The space of the polders strikes the Dutch in various ways. To some, the polders seem an Australia, a limitless

land in which to expand and prosper. To some, they
seem a Sahara, monotonous and sere. Some can't stand
the wide, open spaces, the lack of variation in the landscape, the long roads running through endless fields with
every now and then a farm looking exactly like the farm
several miles back, with everything fulfilling a function,
no ornament anywhere. There are people in Holland who
need crowds, need elbows in their ribs and a sense of
constant crush and turmoil. But there are those, too, who
are willing to move, say, to Lelystad, putting up with
its pioneer and spartan newness in return for the surrounding emptiness, which strikes them as wonderful.
They have also to put up with town planning and architecture that is suddenly uncertain of the way to cope
with all this space. In Lelystad, development of the new
town has begun (a kilometer or so away from the
IJsselmeer, as if no one was quite sure whether or not the
town should be by the water) with tight squares of
poorly designed townhouses—the one toilet in the house
on the ground floor, by the front door; the washroom on
the second floor; and the clotheslines, to which wet
laundry would have to be taken, on a third-floor balcony.
In the village of Nagele, the reaction has been in
the other direction—in a sort of imitative expansiveness.
At least that is the way I saw it. The Dutch architectural
critic R. Blijstra writes about Nagele (which was designed by Dutch members of the architectural group
C.I.A.M.): "The village has . . . been interpreted here as
an interior. An effort has been made to group the elements of this village in such a way that the feeling of

togetherness in a communal area becomes as it were
tangible. . . . An attempt has been made to use the
mechanism of a village pictorially. . . ." However, a page
later in his book *Town-planning in the Netherlands since
1900*, Mr. Blijstra descends from these pictorial heights
to admit that Nagele appears "somewhat emptier" than
other polder villages. In the polder landscape, emptiness
doesn't seem to be a very positive contribution. In reaction to the density of old Dutch cities, these modern
Dutch architects have produced a village that is a
vacuum.

Southern Flevoland had just risen above the water
when I first came to it. It was a black glistening pancake, in one place steaming with mist, in others still wet
in remaining pools. It was probably seven or eight hundred years since this land had been seen before, and
interesting things have been found on it: wrecked ships,
old anchors, and not such old planes. Fourteen hundred
allied bombers came down over this part of Holland during the Second World War, and quite a few have turned
up in the drained polders of the IJsselmeer. In the
wreckage of one Flying Fortress a camera was found
intact. The film, developed, showed a German city from
20,000 feet. Here in the last pools of southern Flevoland
fishnets were strung out to catch the last fish, while
where the soil was already dry enough the first vegetation was sprouting—a yellow-green plant called fleawort,
which looks like Brussels sprouts gone to seed. In one
spot I walked down the face of the dike and felt the
sandy, muddy, peaty ground; it was soft and springy

like grey rubber. It gave me an Adam-like feeling—I was the first man to set foot here, at least since the fourteenth-century inundations, and I could imagine the thrill a Dutchman would have. The fleawort is followed by colts-foot, a plant with large, coarse, grey-green leaves, and then the new soil is sewn with reed, half a kilo of reed seed per acre being scattered from small planes and helicopters. The reed crowds out the fleawort, coltsfoot, and other weeds, and forms a rich humus from the mud. The reed also absorbs a great deal of water, enabling it to evaporate, and then, when all the water in the soil is gone, it loses its vitality and can easily be cut down and burned. The second year the soil is deeply plowed. Rape and lucerne, which is a kind of alfalfa, are the first crops. They are followed by flax and corn, winter wheat and summer barley.

In this brand-new countryside natural life flourishes. Of course, everywhere in Holland a profusion of birds and flowers coexists with a profusion of people. In the Randstad the fact of the dunes, cow pasturage, and water everywhere helps a lot: gulls eat the garbage in the canals, birds chirp in every city street, and duck nests have been built in every little park pond. The priority of nature is indicated in the development plans for the polder city of Lelystad, where the prime site for early construction is a fish hatchery. But birds are the favored heirs of the new land. Gulls come in from the coast while it is being drained, together with terns, avocets, plovers, and oystercatchers. Bees, midges, and flies colonize the reed swamps, and the pools and marsh are soon thick with rails, reed warblers, marsh hens, coots, swans, ducks, and grebe. Mice and voles arrive and encourage the presence of buzzards, kestrels, and harriers. When the reed is burned or gathered for thatch, and cereal and grass cultivation spreads, the lapwings, wagtails, and skylarks fly in. In the grassy fields godwit, redshank, and ruff begin to feed. Pheasants nest in copses and woody plantations, as do pigeons and long-eared owls.

I spent an afternoon with Menno Brandsma, a young biologist who works for the IJsselmeer authority in Kampen, which is an ancient Zuider Zee port. Mr. Brandsma has been following the shifts and changes of nature in the new polders. He said: "We've found that by leaving reeds in certain areas we'll then get birch and alder woods, and consequently pigeons and pheasants nesting in them. Because the water is no longer salt, grass spreads down the sandy beaches—so ruffs are shorebirds here. Eels have been encouraged to come in to reduce the mosquito larvae, which has increased with the conversion of the salt Zuider Zee to the fresh-water IJsselmeer. The eels swim all the way from their breeding grounds in the Sargasso Sea and seem to flourish just as well in fresh water, though our smoked-eel connoisseurs say they aren't quite what they were. The eels are in demand not only with fishermen but with cormorants— and the cormorants are in trouble these days. The fishermen do all they can to get rid of them—they feel the birds are their competitors—and the cormorants also like a lot of sea room, which they no longer have. They're also a bit lazy. We're trying to make a safe home for them in the north corner of East Flevoland. Swans are a problem too. They're settling on the border lakes, and their excreta increases the nitrogen content of the water and encourages pollution. However, we think the bulrush—*Scirpus lacustris*—helps clean it up. We're planting it along the border lakes, especially near campsites where pollution is strong. We've had plagues of shrews, voles, and mice, so we're doing everything we can to encourage the kestrels to stay around, like building nesting boxes for them. A kestrel needs about ten mice a day. We've been following the progress of the mole as he makes his way in from the old land to the new. Earthworms came in with dung from the old land. We think a lot of poor-quality grasses arrived the same way. Some native Israeli plants have appeared in fields of lucerne, sewn with seeds from Israel. We've also discovered some rare birds, like black-winged stilts and dotterels. The dotterel is a white, grey, and brown plover which generally lives on high bare ground in the Scandinavian tundra or the Russian steppes. But for some reason it seems to have decided that our Holland polders, ten feet below sea level, are as good as northern places four thousand feet above sea level. We're trying to look after the dotterels—we've been showing pictures of their nests to farmers, and asking them not to use insecticide close by if they find one. The dotterels like the flax and sugar-beet fields, although when the polders are all under cultivation they may leave us."

By serving nature well, one also serves man. The bor-

der lake has the immediate purpose of being a drain-off
reservoir for the higher old land. Without the lake, the
new land would become too wet every now and then.
But the lake also makes a place to sail, fish, and swim,
and it is a relieving feature in an otherwise uncompro-
mising landscape. There is no "landscaping" because it
is all the effect of necessity, and there is certainly no
beautification (a word which has a cosmetic, camouflag-
ing ring to it); but the Dutch have found that in building
a dike they can use displaced sand to make a beach in
front of it. Dredging a lake deep enough for barge navi-
gation, they can dump the spoil in one spot and make an
island. Mr. Brandsma took me to a place where men had
stood on the polder dike in a high wind and had thrown
willow seeds into the air. The seeds had fallen on the
island, whose soft mud had originally been too dangerous to set foot on, and there were now willows growing
on its firmer soil. The island, moreover, was now a bird
sanctuary.

The straight lines of the Dutch landscape are an expression of what is there. It is a land for the most part
without contours. Bends and curves imposed by man
would not be functional. Beauty in Holland is thus the
result of doing what has to be done as simply and directly as possible with the available materials. Few
things are more beautiful than one of the narrow roads
that run along a polder dike. The road caps the dike.
Trees line the road, giving it shade, breaking the wind,
their roots helping to hold the dike together. Because
the clay and sand of the dike settle unevenly, a road

paved with concrete or asphalt would soon lump and crack. So the road is paved with bricks. The bricks are laid by hand, by men crawling backwards on their knees, tapping the bricks one by one into place in a bed of sand.

❧ 13 ❧

LIKE "FOOTBALL" AND "PIN-UP," "camping" is now an international word. In Holland, as in most other European countries, it is what people do in summer. Along the border lakes of the IJsselmeer camping sites are being made. They are also being set up in great numbers elsewhere in Holland, behind the Zeeland dams, by the Frisian lakes, and in the woods of Gelderland. In May many of the inhabitants of Katwijk and vicinity move into the camping site in the dunes, making their own homes available for rent to Germans. For a while we lived in Lunteren in the bungalow of a schoolteacher's widow, who had moved out to a caravan on a camping site in the woods. All Europe seems to get on the move in July and August, with tents and sleeping bags and other nomadic paraphernalia, and in Holland there are inner and outer migrations, as people from abroad come to Holland, people in Holland go abroad, people in the east of the country go to the west and those in the west go east. The painter-sculptor-architect Constant Nieuwenhuys has written: "Paradoxically enough, when people trek *en masse* to the great outdoors, the difference between town and country disappears. A camping area is a form, however primitive, of a city."

Certainly, loneliness of a Walden variety is not what the Dutch seem to be looking for when they go camping. Nor is the desire to be primitive and nomadic more than an initial impetus that gets one out of the house and into a car jammed with wife, children, tent, cots, trunk, stove, water jugs, blankets, lamps, bicycles, folding boats, and food to last the first week. "In the year 1964 approximately 2.5 million campers visited the over 2800 camp sites in the Netherlands, spending a total of 20 million nights," writes a Dutch authority in a governmental publication, *Environmental Health in the Netherlands* "Seventeen per cent of these were accounted for by visitors from abroad. The campers, who are usually quite inexperienced, have to adapt themselves physically and mentally to an unfamiliar environment, sometimes with a very high density of occupation. A bill went before the Dutch Parliament in 1966 to regulate in camping sites the amount of ground per camper, sleeping accommodation, the supply of drinking water and water for washing, washing accommodation, toilet accommodation, discharge of waste water, storage and disposal of solid waste, etc." A form, perhaps increasingly less primitive, of a city.

I visited some Dutch friends who were camping on Schiermonnikoog, an ex-whaling island off the Frisian coast, which has a winter population of eight hundred and a summer population of nearly five thousand. They were camping a little reluctantly, because the summer cottage they were used to renting for July wasn't available; but after two weeks they felt more or less broken-in, and Mr. Martin Vonkeman, who is a schoolteacher in the town of Drachten, seemed to be taking pleasure in the general good order of things—a pleasure enhanced by their recovery from a storm two nights before which had laid half the camp flat. On Schiermonnikoog two thousand campers camp on a single large site. Even on a grey, blustery day it is a vivid spectacle of colored tents, washing hanging out on clotheslines, and kites flying—all dipping and flapping in the wind, and the sides of the tents beating in and out like canvas lungs. The tents are pitched close together in the dips and hollows of the sand. "They have to concentrate the campers," said Mr. Vonkeman, as we walked around, "otherwise it would be a rambling mess all over the island. The government owns this land and leases it to the camping manager. He allots the sites —next year we've reserved one over there in the lee of those small trees."

The trees form one edge of the site, and on another side are several wooden buildings containing showers, toilets, laundry, and a canteen. Lean-to sheds provide storage for trunks and suitcases. Parking areas and racks are reserved for bikes and *brommers*. The tents face the direction their owners choose, back to the wind or faces to the sun, and are held down by lines and guy wires, which make walking in the area on the impromptu paths and lanes a hazardous procedure. Most tents are surrounded by small private drainage ditches designed to carry water well away from the tent, and to ensure, particularly, that rain doesn't run under the ground cloth. Some tents have separate canvas screens set at an angle across their entrances, for privacy or wind protection, though in fact affording very little of either. People pick their way around the tents, stepping over pegs and lines and outstretched sunbathers. Standing up outside a tent to get the crick out of your neck, you can't help looking into two or three other tents. Moreover, many of the bigger tents have large vinyl picture windows sewn into the canvas walls. There are no windowsills to stand plants on—and whether or not the neighbor back home is remembering to go in and water the plants is the constant anxiety of every Dutch camping family. Here an assortment of wildflowers from the Schiermonnikoog dunes has been placed in a tin cup and put beside the Camping Gaz stove on the folding table. Babies crawl through the sand and can be heard, crying. Large families have a large, central tent and one or two smaller *kinder* tents alongside. Transistor radios bring in all the stations from Hilversum to Hamburg. Clearly, what began as an attempt to have a cheap holiday has become less cheap as one felt the need of a fancier tent, a two-ring gas stove instead of the Primus, more solid camp beds, and all the accessories advertised in the camping magazines to which the family subscribes.

"We feel free out here," said Mr. Vonkeman, not altogether convincingly, as he offered me a campstool outside his tent and sat down himself on the corner of a massive green steamer trunk which also functioned as the Vonkeman pantry. He added, honestly, "Well, we are closer to nature. We walk on the beach, in the dunes, and through the woods. Plenty of fresh air, and sun at least one day out of five."

Mrs. Vonkeman came stooping out of the tent, bearing the coffeepot, looking as if she'd seen enough damp sandy clothes to last the season. She said, "We're still getting over the storm we had the other night when the tent blew down. One thing we learned was that in this sand wooden pegs hold better than metal ones."

❧

Asked where, ideally, they would like to live, most of the Dutch will say, "In the woods." Mr. Vonkeman hopes to live in the woods near Lunteren when he retires from teaching. People who work in the Randstad have as their great ambition the idea of a house—even a little cottage —in the woods of the Veluwe. The Veluwe is a wide belt of sandy soil ("bad soil," one farmer told me) running through the central province of Gelderland. Part of it, the Hooge Veluwe, which is some fourteen thousand acres of woodland and heath, is open only to paying visitors, but the entire area is accessible by road and path, footpaths, cycle tracks, bridle paths, and *brommer* ways, nicely camouflaged with shrubs and trees. One of the best museums in the country, the Kröller-Müller, with its famous Van Gogh collection and extensive sculpture gardens, is situated in the Hooge Veluwe, and there are many other facilities scattered through the woods—swimming pools (here called *bosbaden*), camps, restaurants, playing fields, and riding stables. For though Holland has less recreation space per capita than England or the United States, it uses intensively what it has. Moreover, the amount of Dutch woodland has been increased by the Forest Service from 5 per cent of the area of the country at the end of the nineteenth century to 8 per cent today. The Forest Service encourages use of the woods, planting recreation spots in the poorest timber-growing areas, and elsewhere ensuring that commercial forestry doesn't inhibit vacationers or day-trippers, who might otherwise be driving on the crowded roads or sitting on already packed beaches. Well-designed maps let walkers know where they are in the woods. Small shelters offer cover in storms or showers. Although boar roam in the Hooge Veluwe, and falcons fly, these woods are in no way a wilderness. Indeed, C. H. J. Maliepaard, a Dutch planner, says: "On Monday morning the red deer in this park are so exhausted from running from cover to cover on the previous Sunday, they can be considered the most fanatical opponents of recreation." In the woods near Lunteren I had the impression that if I had felt lost, all I would have needed to do was light a fire. Immediately several Dutchmen would have run up to tell me that fires were not permitted in the woods.

As important for "recreation" needs are the woods of the Randstad cities—and in terms of looks, or general greenery and boskiness, I preferred them to their sandier eastern cousins. The Dutch park has traditionally been more of a wood than an English or North American city park. That in The Hague is called the Bos; it is the place where seventeenth-century burghers used to stroll, admiring the horses and carriages of their wealthier brethren. In Haarlem, the woods and tall trees surrounding the deer pens and duck ponds are what seem most characteristic of the Haarlemner Hout park. Because the Common Market has created a situation where certain crops can be grown more cheaply in other European countries, some Dutch agricultural land is being converted into woods, and in the National Planning Policy, twenty-eight centers of day recreation are recommended, close to major cities, with woods an important part of them. Work has already begun on one such park between Haarlem and Amsterdam. It will form a rural buffer zone between these cities, which are only fifteen minutes apart by train and car, and also a place to which city residents can come without too much planning, if they have a day or an afternoon to spare.

The model to be taken into account in the design of all the wooded parks the Dutch are building now is the Amsterdamse Bos—the Amsterdam Forest Park or, more colloquially perhaps, "the Woods." Like many similar amenities in Holland, the Woods were created from scratch or, rather, from three polders thirteen feet below sea level. It was the good idea of the burgomaster and aldermen of Amsterdam in 1928, and work actually began in 1934 as a means of relieving unemployment. Through the Woods an extensive network of drainage pipes had to be laid to maintain the correct water level in the subsoil so that trees took proper root. But lakes necessary for drainage purposes were also necessary for swimming, canoeing, and simply for their presence as water. First dug was a rowing course. The steep polder dikes were given more gentle slopes so that they seemed less like walls. The construction of a hill was begun. All sorts of trees common to northwestern Europe were planted, covering nearly a thousand of the total two thousand two hundred and thirty acres. The result now, thirty-five years later, is something like the parks one sees in eighteenth-century English portraits, where country gentlemen and their families stand before a sylvan background of deer browsing in sunny clearings or by quiet pools. There are long, wooded slopes, and open glades; here and there a man fishing; a young man and a girl riding by on bicycles, holding hands; some Icelandic ponies ambling through the trees.

At least these were the suggestions on a weekday afternoon in May when I cycled through the Woods with Mr. Heuvelman, the Woods director—he, with generous hospitality, riding a bike borrowed from an assistant so that he could lend me his own reliable machine, a massive, upright black Simplex, made in Amsterdam, with a very hard saddle labeled Hygeia No. 1. "It's one thing now," said Mr. Heuvelman, as we coasted down a slope to the Bosbaan rowing course, where European championships are often held, "but you should see the Woods on summer weekends when over a hundred thousand Amsterdammers are here. The city people love these

Woods. The big trouble is that so many of them now have cars, and five thousand cars is more than we have room to park—we're having to widen the roads in the Woods, and that detracts from what we've made."

Mr. Heuvelman, a very tall, statesmanlike figure in his early fifties, pedaled at a brisk clip along the bicycle paths (of which there are thirty-two miles in the Woods), signaling with a hand for right or left turns, returning the waves of men who were cutting grass or replacing the redwood bulkheading of a drainage canal, now and then stopping with a backward pressure on the coaster brake to point out a notable feature of the Woods. Although such parks were in great demand, Mr. Heuvelman said that the present ones wouldn't be enlarged; it was better to build new parks closer to the people who needed them, and with a few contemporary improvements: better access by car, more parking space on the periphery, and perhaps less of a highway through the park—which was one of the design mistakes made with the Woods, but understandable in the 1930's when few recognized how prevalent cars were going to be. He thought the perfect park should be roughly one third woods, one third water, and one third open space. Thus room for birds and flowers, room for waterfowl and water sports, room for picnics and sunbathing and football games. In the Amsterdamse Bos overnight camping is restricted to a small site at the south end, but the woods are never closed. They are patrolled by the police of Amsterdam, Aalsmeer, and Amstelveen, the three municipalities in which the Woods are located, and by eight park rangers with dogs. The crime rate is about the same as in Amsterdam itself. The ground is always a little damp, because the Woods are below sea level, and there are never any forest fires. One failure has been an open-air theater, rarely used because of the noise from planes taking off from Schiphol.

Holland, with its base of sand and water, is a good country for children, and in the Woods there are many specific sites, with more now being built, for children to mix water, sand, and themselves in any quantity. The Dutch genius for the moderate use of things is evident in soccer goal posts with continuous tubular frames, like those of aluminum garden chairs. The posts do not need to be planted in the ground and can be moved anywhere on a field, so that one spot isn't continuously played on and the grass denuded. These posts also make possible a number of impromptu games on one field. Throughout the Woods there are short landing strips, for aircraft emergencies, but these have never been used. Cows graze on them now, the stock of dairy farmers forced off land taken for dormitory developments; the pasture thereby helps not only the farmers but the pastoral atmosphere—in fact the cows I saw were wearing coats, which was not only pastoral but *gezellig*, the word the Dutch use constantly to convey the idea of being warm, comfortable, or cozy. Ducks flew over the road by the canoeing lake, and when Mr. Heuvelman and I paused for a moment on top of a small bridge, not only ducks swam up but half a dozen big black-striped grey carp; they bobbed to the surface in the shadowed reflection of the bridge's arc and begged for food. The recreation grounds were lush green fields (I thought for a moment of those arid stretches of so-called recreation park off the Lower East River Drive in Manhattan, where plenty of water is just as accessible). Many of the men working in the Woods are in some way handicapped, or on probation. There is a clubhouse for handicapped Boy Scouts. There is a stable and ten miles of bridle path, which Mr. Heuvelman said had recently been made narrower by letting trees and bushes grow in on them. The horses prefer a narrow path through the trees.

Hearing a nightingale, we dismounted and left the bikes at the foot of the hill—the man-made hill. We walked up past a bonfire of pruned branches, past a bulldozer parked on the edge of the rough, unfinished plateau of the summit, forty feet above sea level. For the Randstad, a real eminence. "We used this as our soil depot for a long time," said Mr. Heuvelman, "but now we soon hope to have it finished. In winter it will be good for skiing and sledding. In summer it will be good for walking up and sitting on. You see our view. Starting in the west, that's the Schiphol control tower. Then, moving north, those are the floodlights round the rim of the Olympic stadium, and next in the distance the spires and towers of the city—the Westerkerk, the Hilton, the new harbor building, the new Netherlands Bank, the Oudekerk, finally coming round to the apartment blocks in Buitenveldert and the new University hospital. When we get the top on this hill we think people will say that it is worth climbing."

❦

The greenery around Dutch towns and cities grows not only in woods and parks but in allotments—areas given over to thousands of tiny gardens, where city workers can potter in the evenings, raising vegetables or flowers, and whole families spend weekends as if on their country estates. Just outside Amsterdam in the Watergrafsmeer you can see such an allotment city. There the little gardens cluster below a dike, on each garden a small house, actually a garden shed which in the course of evenings and weekends with the accretion of tarpaper, shingles, tiles, and linoleum has become a residence. Here, each man has been his own builder, planner, and architect. Each cottage with its flattish roof and leaning stovepipe is slightly different from the one next door. Small cinder paths lined by trim hedges run between the houses and past white-painted gates to each front door. It is a sort of permanent camping; inside each *huisje* are bunk beds, plywood cupboards, and a Primus stove. There are plants on the windowsills and around each house—the soil is rich black—flowerbeds, for as the garden hut has become a second home so the vegetable patch has become an ornamental garden.

The allotments are taken seriously by most Dutch town-planners. They are not land which can be considered ripe for dormitory exploitation. They are needed the way they are. Amsterdam leased out such allotments on an organized basis in 1909, formalizing the historic use city people had always made of land outside the city walls. Rotterdam has planned its allotments in belts of parkland during recent expansions. Although flat dwellers would seem to be in greatest need of them, people who live in houses want them too. Around The Hague a third of the allotment holders live in houses with gardens and clearly seek more than a place to grow things; they want to be further away from the place where they live most of the time: they want peace and quiet in the open air. But as the space the allotments occupy seems more significant and valuable there are pressures for regulation. It is indicated in sociological studies, which talk of the effect of the allotments in strengthening family ties, acquainting city children with the rhythm of the seasons, and bolstering the community spirit of the allotment holders. The studies go on to note that allotments should be open to the public and have more attention devoted to their general layout. R. Blijstra writes, in "Town Planning in the Netherlands since 1900," (commenting on the research of W. H. Vermooten): "If these groups of allotments are to be made into parks, the little houses on the individual allotments, which are occasionally regarded by foreigners . . . as something of a *bidonville,* i.e., slum dwellings, will have to be improved, which is going to cost money and which will therefore be a serious drawback for many allotment holders. In that case, too, keepers will have to be appointed, and allotment-holders' associations certainly cannot pay the costs of this."

The word *keepers* suggests some of the barbed-wire aspects of the organization of shortage, but there are places in Holland where the very lack of barbed wire is impressive. I frequently drove to The Hague on a road from Katwijk to Wassenaar which passed through a marine camp. It went right through the middle of it, with the barracks on either side of the road. The barracks, in fact, were large bungalows, and were surrounded by cherry trees and flowerbeds. On the west side of the encampment were the dunes and on the east, tulip and hyacinth fields.

I confess to have harbored a desire to write about Holland without writing about tulips, but it is impossible. Tulips are an obsession with the Dutch. They are also a vivid reflection of intensity and tight fit. The flower originally came from the roadsides of Asia Minor, where it was found by the Crusaders. In Turkish monasteries tulips were cultivated to a point where sultans and rich merchants thought the flowers as precious as silks or spices. The name came from there: tulip being a tulband or turban. An Austrian ambassador to Turkey brought the flower to Vienna in 1554. In Vienna the Hapsburg court gardener, a Dutchman, became infatuated and brought tulips back to the Netherlands. There the coarse, sandy soil behind the dunes proved ideal for the propagation of tulips. They became a fashion at the court of Louis XIII, and a fad in Holland. Fashionable painters like Judith Leyster, a pupil of Frans Hals, were commissioned to paint portrait albums of different types of tulips, particularly those affected by a virus which produced wild and brilliant flashes of color. Tulips also became a kind of stock to be gambled in, the object of a nearly nationwide mania which lasted from 1634 to 1638.

In 1637, the great year of tulip madness, the fever reached a pitch where in one town alone ten million guilders changed hands in tulip transactions. One brewer offered his brewery for a single bulb. Some bulbs changed hands several times a day. At an Alkmaar auction on February 5, 1637, where several tulips had asking prices of more than a thousand guilders, a Viceroy tulip was catalogued at 4,203 guilders (Rembrandt's large house in Amsterdam was worth about 8,000 guilders). The historian Paul Zumthor writes: "The few citizens who kept their heads called the rest 'the hooded ones' in allusion to the hoods worn by madmen: they brought out pamphlets and satirical songs whose humor became increasingly bitter." Jan Breughel II, seeing a number of his colleagues ruined in the final crash, painted tulips being cherished by a group of monkeys.

Today sophisticated Hollanders will say: "Oh, those stupid tulips!" but they remain susceptible to the feelings aroused by the dense bands of color which are the tulip and daffodil fields in spring, and by the intoxicating scent that wafts off the hyacinth and narcissus fields. In April and May the roadsides of the bulb district are lined with stalls selling cut flowers. Boys flag down motorists to offer slings of voluptuous daffodils, to be draped over the bonnet of the car. In the way some Americans feel the urge to drive into New England to see fall leaves, the entire Dutch nation is compelled every spring to drive slowly along the *bloembollen* route, a scenic meandering way through the fields, to take trips to the research greenhouses, or to rise at dawn to see the barges bringing the flowers to the Aalsmeer auction market. Not only do they do this themselves, but they have convinced the Germans, British, and increasing numbers of Swiss, Belgians, French, and Italians that life is incomplete without at least once doing the same. However, because tulips are now generally polled a few days after flowering, so that the bulbs retain their sap, colorfully interesting fields are fewer, and the tulip growers have set up an exhibition park, the Keukenhof, near Lisse, where every year ten million bulbs are planted. The result is not only a dense, more permanent display of flowers but an advance of six weeks in the beginning of the tourist season, and delighted restaurant, hotel, and lodging-house keepers in the surrounding towns.

I went to the Keukenhof on a rainy day but, even so, there were thousands of persons streaming along the sixteen kilometers of footpath, holding up umbrellas as they viewed the regiments and battalions of flowers planted under trees and beside little canals, in open beds and in massive greenhouses. On a rainy day the color of the flowers is entirely their own, not aided by the sun; and the moist air brings forth the sweetness of hyacinths and the more subtle scent of narcissi. There are creamy white hyacinths which look like popcorn on a stick—indeed, some heavier-headed hyacinths are held up by steel needles. I admired Greenland, a light green-pink-blue tulip, and the nearly black tulips which have the fascination of difficulty: Black Beauty, Black Pearl, Queen of Night, and Ace of Spades—the last a dusky purple tulip that seemed to turn charcoal if one looked at it long enough. An artist might well be jealous of the audience the Keukenhof flowers have, all those people streaming along in a sensual communion (the girls looking like flowers, the older women somewhat bulb-shaped), all acting as if they were under the influence of a calming, beneficent drug. And indeed here and there along the paths have been placed pieces of modern sculpture, which seem in some ways to serve as foils for the flowers and, in others, to gain distinction and interest from being in nature's presence.

In Haarlem I looked at the private bulb fields of Mr. Thomas Hoog, who has retired from active business as a bulb exporter, but still serves as vice president of the Dutch Tulip Growers Association. Mr. Hoog is a rosy-cheeked man in his sixties who wouldn't look at all out of place in a Hals portrait of the regents of an old people's home, or *hofje*—and who in fact does serve as such a regent. From Mr. Hoog I learned something about the intensive nature of bulb-growing. Twelve thousand growers produce roughly four billion bulbs a year on twenty-five thousand acres. The return is nearly sixty million dollars—a sum that would buy 700,000 tons of wheat, which (grown in Holland) would require 40,000 acres of land. Although much of the business is in forcing bulbs for cut-flower production, the export of bulbs makes up a quarter of Dutch horticultural exports. Germany is the best customer. The English buy too, but they also grow a lot of bulbs of their own. The U.S.S.R. is a blossoming market. The Dutch reclaimed many parts of Russia in the eighteenth and nineteenth centuries and built locks and canals there. In recent years, while other countries have been selling the Russians car-making machinery or power plants, the Dutch have been building huge greenhouses in Moscow for bulb-forcing. Mr. Hoog's sons, who now run the family firm, often make trips to Russia to drum up bulb business. In his front garden Mr. Hoog showed me two tulips with Russian associations—one called Gudoshnik, which means clown, a yellow and red flower; and another called Greig, named after a Scottish admiral who served in the Imperial Russian Navy, a wild-looking vermillion tulip with striped reddish-green leaves. Generals and admirals traditionally give their names to tulips, and among the two thousand contemporary varieties with names that range from Good Gracious to Greta Garbo one also finds Omar Bradley, Simon Bolivar, Eisenhower, and Patton.

But despite the flattery implicit in some of those names, America disappoints Dutch tulip growers. Mr. Hoog said Americans just weren't flower-minded—extensive advertising and promotion hadn't produced any great result. In the United States, moreover, Dutch bulbs were up against Japanese competition, with bulbs that produce flowers similar to Dutch flowers being sold at very low prices on the West Coast. Mr. Hoog, however, believed that in the long run Dutch reliability would pay off wherever a serious market existed. A Dutch firm lacking bulbs of its own would buy from a competitor and ship them at a loss, while Japanese firms shipped nothing and lost the business. Japan was also too dry in summer, and the dryness caused virus infections in the bulbs. Mr.

Hoog showed me a painting of a tulip in one of his great treasures—a tulip catalog painted by Judith Leyster—which had the violent streaks associated with a virus. Such bulbs (although particularly valued in the seventeenth century), are not sought after now, for it has since been found that the infection produces smaller and smaller bulbs. Nowadays only two growers purposely produce the inflamed bulbs, and any that crop up elsewhere are shipped to the bulb laboratory at Lisse for observation.

There is, perhaps, something in the matter of a lot of people being forced to become good gardeners by the exigencies of space and their distaste for chaos that makes one think of Japan. And perhaps there are times when the Dutch, too, seem to have their share of inscrutability. But I think one can guess what is in the mind of the man one sees pacing slowly around his empty bulb fields on a Sunday morning, all the daffodils cut, looking at the ground as he steps along with a relaxed and happy concentration: all this is mine—I have this and that to do—and next April they will grow again. The ground in these Randstad fields has been made as perfect for the purpose as possible, with the surface sand removed to a depth of seventy centimeters above the water table, leaving a layer of coarse sand with some chalk in it to which every year manure is added to give it humus. Within the ground the water level can be controlled so that it is neither too wet in winter nor too dry in summer. The growers pay special rates to the Rijnland Waterschaap in Leiden, which handles this delicate and absolutely essential matter, generally pumping in extra water in April and, in autumn, in preparation for winter rains, lowering the level of the surrounding canals. So far salt has not affected this most valuable Randstad harvest, but several farmers have had their tulips affected by fumes from the chemical works and iron foundries at IJmuiden. Fume-resistant strains are being developed, but, in the meantime, Mr. Hoog helped to arrange for compensation to be paid.

❦ 14 ❦

IN A SHORT LIST of truly relevant Dutch statistics, among the numbers of birds, births, and bicycles, would have to be the fact that there is one cow for every three people; in 1967 there were 4,018,957 cows. Until I went to Holland, cows were one branch of the tree of life about which I felt no particular curiosity. They were useful objects to point out to children in the course of a boring car ride: "Look, cows." But in Holland you soon get pretty tired of pointing out cows. Even in the Randstad they seem to be everywhere you look, and if there aren't any live cows around, as there may not be in the center of a city or town, when it isn't market day, then there will probably be a statue of a cow, like that in the square at Leeuwarden, or in front of the station in

Groningen where there is a sculpture of an amply proportioned nude woman standing with one foot on a kneeling calf. One of the Dutch masterpieces (whose value sometimes seems set a trifle high to other people) is Paul Potter's "The Bull," which hangs in The Mauritshuis in The Hague—an ingenuous, painstaking representation of an almost sacred animal.

If you exclude the water-covered areas, some 70 per cent of Holland is used for farming. Although this may be the highest proportion of a country in agricultural use anywhere in the world, what is more significant is that most of it is farmed more intensively than elsewhere. In fact, it is reckoned that the world could sustain between twelve and fifteen billion people if methods of cultivation and soil preservation were everywhere brought up to Dutch standards. Nevertheless, the Dutch produce only two thirds of what they eat—the rest, mostly crops that can't be economically grown in Holland, has to be imported. And though the Netherlands provides other countries with eggs, bacon, pork, beef, lettuce, vegetables, fruit and flowers, and of course dairy products, agriculture now forms only 10 per cent of the Dutch economy. The number of farms is shrinking (from 199,785 in 1960 to 162,230 in 1967), though the average size is growing, together with the number of cows and the annual milk production. Farmers need larger farms and more cows to be prosperous; their realization of this has assisted government subsidized reparceling schemes. However, Holland has no crop failures, and one result right now of this efficient, intensive farming is that the country has a large surplus of cheese and butter. The Dutch themselves do not drink much milk and they buy the cheaper margarine.

The pre-eminent cow and milk province is Friesland, a province of wet green fields and wide lakes and huge barns, a province where there are as many cows as there are people. In Friesland some farms are fancy. I saw one, near Wierum, built in the fairly common head-neck-and-body style, with a new house and barn connected by a corridor, and all covered with thatch so trim that it seemed to have been carefully combed. There was painted scrollwork on the gate and front door, and sitting apart on the clipped lawn of the *terp*, or artificial mound raised above the floodable fields, a small thatched gazebo. Most Fries farms have house and barn under the same vast roof. If the roof isn't thatched, it is covered with large glazed tiles which in sunlight look as if maple syrup has been poured over them and is running down the steep slope.

At Oldeboorn, a village with roughly fifteen hundred people and a hundred farms, I spent a day with the Heerma family. Enneus Heerma, who is a student of political science at the University of Amsterdam, met me in the village and guided me to his family's farm on the Prikweg, a narrow road along which for several miles farmhouses are built on alternate sides every few hundred yards. Enneus (the Dutch form of Aeneas, a classical name as much used in Holland as Homer is in America) told me that since the floods in 1460 or thereabouts all the land in this area had been under water, and frozen most winters. In summer, farmers had come and pitched tents while they gathered a quick crop of hay. In the 1930's nearly a third of the farmers in the area emigrated, for the most part to Canada and Australia, and during the war, the region had been considered by the Germans so remote and useless that the RAF dropped supplies to the Dutch resistance there. After the war, a small polder was created with the help of funds given by Queen Wilhelmina and the labor of men who would have otherwise been unemployed. In the 2,500 acres thus reclaimed some thirty farms were made. Most are owned by the state and leased out; some are owned by private people. Enneus' older brother, Gerrit, has a state-owned farm on the Prikweg, while his father used to own his own farm but sold it to a private individual and now leases it back. Mr. Heerma runs his farm himself, with the year-round help of his wife and the help in summer of an agricultural student. Enneus does the books when he comes home for the weekend.

The Heermas' house occupies about a third of the space under the farm roof. Downstairs there is a kitchen-dining room, a living room, and a shower; upstairs, three bedrooms. In the back hall (which also gives access to the barn and contains the three-ring gas cooker on which Mrs. Heerma prepares the meals) one leaves one's boots or wooden shoes before going into the dining room. It is solid farmers' fare: a little meat, lots of potatoes and gravy. Mr. Heerma, a stooped, bright-eyed, hollow-cheeked man in his late fifties, says grace beforehand in Fries and afterward reads from the Bible in Dutch.

Religion outlines much of the Heerma family life, and the cows dominate the rest. There are twenty in the herd, as many as can be kept on the Heermas' thirty-five acres. They are milked twice a day, from five to seven in the morning, and from four to six in the afternoon. One of the dining-room drawers has the important cow papers in it, and Mr. Heerma is proud to point out that, on a 100 point basis, most of his cows are graded in the 70's and 80's. His cows have such names as Gerda, Barbara, Eminent Fetje, Sam's Barbara, and Diamant's Eke. The word *cow* is the same in Fries and in English. After it is two years old a cow can have a calf, and thereafter it calves every year and produces milk ten months of the year. When a calf is born, Mr. Heerma writes down that fact on a calendar hanging in the cow-shed, and when Enneus is home, the proper forms are filled out so that the calf is listed in the central cow registration book at Leeuwarden. Cows catch cold and get infections—the more milk they make, the less resistance they seem to have; and the windows in the Heerma cowshed are arranged so that drafts don't blow on the underside of the cows when they're being milked. The cows have moods like women. During its monthly period, when it tends to be a little upset, Mr. Heerma keeps the cow in the barn, and the cow's friends—cows generally take up the same position in the fields day after day and seem very faithful to their chosen companions—get as close to the barn as they can and moo to let the confined cow know they are missing her and are there.

Long before they had a National Planning Policy, the

Dutch were working out what to do with their land. Mr. Heerma has organized all the possibilties of his thirty-five acres, dividing it with small drainage ditches every two feet, running pipes under earthern ridges where tractors have to pass from one such island to the next. There are no walls or hedges—instead, a one-strand electric wire fence which Mr. Heerma picks up live, not minding the jolt, and moves to the next area of grass he wants his cows to eat. The small ditches drain to a larger ditch along the road. This, at the end of the Prikweg, joins a canal leading to the polder pumping station, lined along the route with reed-covered churns for ducks to lay eggs in. The Heerma acreage is kept heavily manured, and fertilized with a nitrogen product, and on it grow two and sometimes three crops of hay for winter use, as well as summer pasturage for the cows. On two sides of the barn Mr. Heerma has planted a line of fast-growing poplars to serve as a windbreak and also to provide shade.

The barn is like a Viking hall inside, with columns and trusses that still have the shape of trees, and beams that often are still bark-covered. Swallows dart under the dusty skylights, and the air smells thick and warm. By midsummer the cut hay is beginning to reach the level of the eaves. Most of the time a powerful fan sends air up through a shaft in the hay, forcing out the heat, which is generated by damp and the hay's weight, and which can cause the hay to catch fire. I put my hand in the stack at one point and the feeling of moist heat was a shock. Enneus said that, in the past, farmers had had

the huge job of pitching the hay outside in fine weather
to relieve the danger, and even so there were many fires.
Even with machine-driven fans, there are still cases of
spontaneous combustion today—in Friesland one fire a
month being unexceptional. (I saw one farm near
Surhuisterveen where the remnants of the hay were
smoldering in the ruins of the barn ten days later.)
Motors also drive the vacuum machine which milks the
cows, and the pump which draws the dung along a concrete channel in the cowshed to a concrete tank beside
the field gate. Without machinery Mr. Heerma wouldn't
be able to deal with twenty cows, and he needs twenty
to make a reasonable living. With a milking machine it
takes four minutes to milk a cow, by hand it takes eight.
Mr. Heerma generally starts the cows by hand and then
switches them to the machine. He shares a tractor with
his son Gerrit, and joins other farmers in the polder in
the rent of harvesting machinery; they all get on very
well with one another except occasionally when one of
them wants, say, a little more water pumped out of the
canal by the Waterschaap official than the other farmers
want. Mr. Heerma, together with all the Oldeboorn dairy
farmers, belongs to a cooperative whose tractor and cart
picks up the milk twice a day from the farm gate, and
whose inspector comes every three weeks to examine the
cows and grade the milk. Mrs. Heerma is in charge of
the farm's quality control; she scrubs the pans and
buckets and milking machine, and gives medicine to sick
cows. Grade A milk fetches a higher price than B or C,
and the Heermas' milk is generally graded A. In terms

of quantity, the Heerma cows also do well. The national average is roughly 4,200 liters per cow per year. In 1967 the Heerma cows produced an average of 4,337 liters.

Life along the Prikweg is intimately bound to the price of milk, which is set by the government every April. In 1967 the price was reduced by two cents a liter, but it is apparently still too high in terms of encouraging the Dutch to drink more milk and buy more butter. From a farmer's point of view, of course, the price can't be too high, and perhaps into the complicated computations that have to be done should be fed some reckoning of the role farms play, not only as milk producers, but as oases of space and greenery and the sustainers of people like the Heermas. That, it would seem to me, would be worth subsidizing. In any case, although life along the Prikweg is easier than it was, it is not a leisured one. The Heermas have a television and a new Opel sedan. The Common Market has helped in many ways: the tractor is German, like the car, and not too expensive; but there is also competition from Italian wheat and Danish butter. Oldeboorn itself is losing a little of its vitality, in the way most Dutch villages are, outside the Randstad. Young people want jobs in the bigger towns and cities. Thirty years ago Oldeboorn had eight bakers—now it has three. Some villages in Friesland are now without a barber, and this is regarded as a sign of real collapse.

Growing up, Enneus and his brother and sister had to cycle daily eighteen kilometers each way to and from high school in Drachten. In afternoons and on Saturdays they did farm chores before playing with children from the other polder farms. In summer they went fishing, looking for lapwing eggs, and rowing and sailing on the Pikermeer. In winter they looked forward to freezing weather so that they could skate. On Saturday evenings the boys and girls gathered in the square and looked each other over; there were dances, and still are— Oldeboorn has a beat group called the Early Birds. But Sundays are the Sabbath. If you aren't in church your neighbors assume you are very ill. The older Heermas never have a vacation; they go to church twice on Sundays, and frown on television that day. Girls do embroidery, and the radio is turned on only for the midday news. Here, where the cows always need milking, wooden shoes are not objects of sentiment. Mr. Heerma has big tennis-ball-like bubbles on the instep of each foot from a lifetime of wearing them.

❦ 15 ❦

IN THE RANDSTAD ONE DREAMS of space or mountains; people long for the Australian outback or the Austrian Tyrol. The dream is present in Dutch paintings of former times, for instance in the mountainous fantasies of Hercules Seghers, and it is there too in Dutch history as one of the motives that drove men from Enkhuisen or Rhenen to Capetown and Sumatra, Timor and Brazil. In every Dutchman there is a bit of the explorer Tasman or of a settler of Nieuw Amsterdam. Although on a graph emigration reached one peak in the 1930's and a second in the 1950's, and has been going down steadily ever since, the Dutch still emigrate. But crowded, prosperous Holland provides for those who stay several ways for embodying such dreams and for finding space and silence. I spent several weeks on a yacht—the word is originally Dutch—cruising through the canals and lakes of Friesland and the wider waters of the IJsselmeer, learning to appreciate the fact that in Holland the wind blows most of the time, making what felt like arduous voyages of half a dozen kilometers daily from one village to another, negotiating such perilous obstacles as bridges which were sometimes reluctant to open, and barges which seemed to swell as they approached, taking up the entire navigable channel and making a bow wave which threatened to lift our thirty-foot steel sloop over the canal bank into the nearest field.

Such man-made perils exist, together with constant meteorological apprehensions; but from a boat Holland is a park bestowing traditional, natural blessings. You can sail into what elsewhere would be the main street of a small town and here is the main canal, and—mooring there—become for a day or two part of that town's life. You are a citizen of the water. Children will call on you, and old men will show you where the key to the public water-tap is kept. The man who runs the opening bridge will tell you how many barges he has let through since Easter and how far road traffic backs up on a summer

Sunday when all the yachts come by. On the water people still wave to one another, perhaps because they share an element on which they may need each other's help. There are no landlords on the water, and you can change neighbors by lifting your mooring lines. And if you like, you can sail onto a large lake and down a side channel into a smaller lake and there, choosing for comfort the windward shore and a spot marked on the chart with a few inches more water than your yacht draws, you can plump the apple-cheeked steel bows into the soft bank of mud, topped with tall grass. There you can spend an evening or, if you are well supplied, a week.

Before I met the Heermas, I spent three days moored in this manner in the edge of a field not far from Olde-boorn. It is the longest I have ever spent in such a seemingly restricted spot. The field, a foot or so above lake level, was bounded by unbridged and unjumpable ditches. A few small trees grew near the dent, or bay, into which we had run the boat and made our own smaller dent in the bank. We had an anchor out in the high grass and a stern line to the trunk of the strongest-looking tree. In the distance were the circus-tent shapes of the barns. Now and then another yacht sailed astern of us down the lake or along a more distant reach of water, so that all we could see were the sails moving above the grass. If the wind was right we sometimes heard a train or a tractor. Otherwise the noise was that of wind and cows and birds. Our universe had shrunk to strange new proportions, but far from being bored the children built a house out of grass, played a perpetual game of hide-and-seek in the field, fell into the dirtiest of the ditches, and swam with no ill-results in the peaty, coffee-colored water of the little bay. It was the sort of place that would turn the most nervous, urban individual into a naturalist. Many of the Dutch are pigeon-fanciers, photographers of flowers, or members of Artis, the Amsterdam Zoological Society, and Holland is a country where the ability to tell one flower or bird from another comes to seem not just worthwhile but essential, a kind of respect and concentration demanded by the environment.

Wildflowers in our field were there to be identified. Birds came and the only thing was to learn how to tell oystercatcher from lapwing, godwit from ruff. There are always cows and always ducks, but I can perhaps suggest the benign mood induced in that spot by mentioning what really delighted us one evening, when the wind had dropped and the family of ducks that had been attending us had departed, looking for a change of diet. This was the arrival of some grebes. They were three— mother, father, and child, graceful diving birds with longer necks than ducks, and tailless bodies riding lower in the water. The infant grebe sat perched amid the ruffled feathers of his mother's back, and only descended from this *gezellig* spot to swim toward his father, who was returning from a successful dive. The infant took the proffered fish in open bill; then swallowed it, gulping, though the fish was little smaller than himself. He shook his head a couple of times and swam back to mama, who was still cruising placidly in the little bay. When he reached her, the small grebe scrambled with a good deal of fluttering up his mother's back and resumed his seat.

❦

Sailing is one way. Walking, I thought, might be another method of finding space, silence, and no signposts in Holland—walking, for instance, to Schiermonnikoog (the island where my friends the Vonkemans camp), one of what Sir William Temple calls finely "the broken remainders of a continued Coast," the chain of islands running along this margin of Holland, Germany and Denmark, and in the Dutch section separated from the mainland by the Waddenzee. *Wadden* means shallows. The word has the same root as the English *wade*, and a friend in The Hague told me there was a Dutch word *wadlopen* which meant precisely that: to wade or walk through the shallows of the Waddenzee from the mainland coast to the islands. Although it sounded to me like the kind of sport you might just invent if no other sports were available, and you were desperate, my informant said it was an adventure. He added that it was also very dangerous, and one should take a guide.

My personal case of flat neurosis, acquired in Katwijk, was thus finally cured about a third of the way across the Waddenzee, when the dike of the Nine Farmers polder on the Groningen shore had disappeared in the fog, the dunes of Schiermonnikoog were invisible, an alleged eight or nine kilometers to the north, and I was plodding slowly through shin-deep mud (that was liberally laced with shells) toward my guide, the moment before up to his neck in a tide-filled gully, and now returning from reconnoitering a shallower crossing place. Let me recommend the cure. Let me also say that although I went *wadloping* with the idea of finding isolation, wildness, and no people, I wasn't disappointed when I found that those were not the benefits one got from the sport. There were other things.

In the thirteenth century Cistercian monks from Claerkamp, near Dokkum, are said to have taken their cattle across the Wad for pasture on Schiermonnikoog —which means, in Fries, island of the grey monks. In the years since, people have sometimes ventured out onto the mud to get straying cattle, but generally the farmers of the Frisian shore have a fearful respect for what lies beyond the dike. There are too many tales of people setting out and getting lost in the fog or exhausted and stuck in the mud: sometimes their bodies were found. Since the Second World War, however, the coastal village of Pieterburen has been sponsoring the sport of *wadlopen*. Some of the fees paid to Pieterburen guides have helped to restore the village church and mill, and to keep up the botanical garden. Local men have trained students at Groningen University and similar young enthusiasts as guides. They have had to traverse all the routes to the islands, crossing the various channels and gullies, learning the few landmarks and seamarks and the character of tides and currents, and eventually making a solo lope to prove their worth.

I reached Pieterburen at nine o'clock one Saturday morning in July, after driving down miles of narrow lanes which weaved along the ancient boundaries of fields. In Pieterburen, a mile or so in from the coast, a hundred people were gathered in and around the Wappen van Huizingoo Inn. They were of both sexes, all ages, and all were erstwhile *wadlopers*. Dick van der Zee, a tall, bearded geography graduate student from Groningen who was one of the guides, told me that two thousand people had already gone *wadloping* that season, including a few Germans and one Australian who was hitchhiking from London to Stockholm and stopped off in Pieterburen to get in what he called some real walking. The Dutch *wadlopers* had included parties of high school girls, 20 paratroopers on maneuvers, and quite a lot of middle-aged executives. People who worked at desks, thinking, were more eager to *wadlope* than people like farmers or builders who already worked in the open air. Van der Zee said that the only people who hadn't completed the trip this year were a Chilean couple from Paris. A few hundred yards from the dike, they took a long look at the mud and decided not to go on. He preferred them to the occasional person who got about a third of the way across before changing his mind, and then had to be assisted back to the mainland.

Buses carried us several kilometers west of Pieterburen and deposited us in a farmyard half a mile from the shore. "Shore," however, here needs defining. We first came to the "sleeper," an old sea dike which was now a reserve dike protecting a polder. After walking along this dike for a way we turned northward across a newer polder, full of wheat, bounded by the most recent and most seaward of the dikes. Under the forward slope of this were several green aprons of new land, as yet un-diked, called *kwelder*. They were covered with green turf and were slowly being formed as the result of rows of wickerwork fencing and crisscross ditches farmers had built there. The farmers' sheep grazed on the *kwelder*, fertilizing and compressing the new soil. In the meantime the dike on which we stood was the southern limit of the Wad, and looking out we had a view of it at low tide—an expanse of dull brown and black waffle-iron flats. There were low grey skies, and a thin grey drizzle borne on a not particularly warming northeast wind. Schiermonni-koog was invisible. Van der Zee said it was ten kilo-meters north, but it would be about fifteen by the route we were going to take. There was some brightness in the green of the *kwelder*, and the red, yellow, and orange parkas worn by some of the *wadlopers*. Everyone wore shorts and sneakers, preferably the high-sided basketball kind, and most people carried a knapsack or airline bag containing lunch and a change of clothes.

We had an easy first hundred yards along the top of an experimental dike being built at right-angles to the shore. Then, with a sudden *thuck*, we were in the real thing. Not showing much aggressiveness to be first in the mud, I found myself in the last of five parties that formed, each with a guide—in our case, van der Zee. He carried a staff, for use as a stretcher pole if needed, and a first-aid kit and a compass, which as rearguard he wasn't going to need unless fog rolled in. Although it was low tide, the northeasterly wind had pushed in more water than usual, and for a while we walked with an effort in mud that felt like molasses and was covered with eighteen inches of the North Sea. There was little talking except for an occasional oath, laugh, or exclamation. It was three-dimensional walking, up and down as well as forward, a bit like riding a bicycle—though you had to pull your feet up rather than push them down, using your ankles and soon feeling it in the thighs, as if you'd been climbing an endless, steep Dutch staircase. The Sisyphean aspects were relieved a little by the sounds of water parting and mud sucking and the splash of someone missing his step and lurching off balance. Cries of *"Zwarte Piet!"* greeted the black of face or bottom. In the afterguard, watching the antics of those ahead, we had a better chance to pick the least perilous path, but even so we had our adventures. In one piece of above-water going we were forced to cross a muddy dip. Some tried running, and some a sort of hop, skip, and jump, but there seemed to be no method which didn't get you covered with mud at least to the thighs. It was in all cases important to keep moving. Anyone who faltered or changed plans in mid-dip got a leg stuck, and in trying to pull it out, toppled over, getting his arms in the mud as well. It was also important not to fear the mud, and to realize that the more surface you presented to the mud the less chance it had of dragging you down—flat-outstretched would be best. The successful *wadloper* clearly liked mud, its smell, its color, its texture. Once you had a thick coating, it seemed to matter less.

After an hour or so we reached a mussel bank and

rested. The bank lay on the edge of one of the fingers of a channel which came in like an arm around the eastern end of Schiermonnikoog and almost reached the outstretched fingers of the channel which curved around the western end. Most of the channels still have water in them at low tide, and their winding courses are marked by buoys or thin, branchless saplings stuck in the mud at every bend. From the mainland to the island runs a ridge, the *wantij*, or watershed, which keeps east and west channels from joining up, though some of their tributaries cut into it and form gullies that even at low tide can be surprisingly deep with water. At high tide, which comes faster and higher in certain weathers that the expert *wadloper* learns to recognize, the Wad is covered by at least six feet of salt water.

It was nearly low water when we reached the mussel bank, after two hours of walking. From the bank the Wad looked like a sheet of coarse wet sandpaper, the abrasive bumps being small hills made by sand-worms. Here and there stood birds: shelduck, terns, avocets, and oyster catchers, which the Dutch call *bontepiet*. Sometimes there are seals. Van der Zee led me to see the three-foot-high cliff on one side of the gully where various strata of mud, sand, and clay were exposed, occasionally interspersed with a layer of shells. Coming down to the gully were miniature rivers and miniature deltas, with morainelike deposits, and van der Zee pointed out how even these smallest channels of the Wad followed the pattern of large rivers by being deepest on the outside of the bends. The mud itself changed

color, getting blacker as it got deeper—a result of less
oxygen reaching its content of sulphur. In one channel
tiny shrimp could be scooped up as they flowed past.
The water was still running east, the last of the ebb.

We began walking again. One of the men in our party
handed round some dried prunes and another offered
everyone a Fam peppermint. Ahead of us the other four
groups were spread out—they made a surrealistic sight,
plodding forward over the dried-out sea. Some walked
by themselves, some in small bunches, some alongside a
chance acquaintance, talking about what they saw or
about themselves, the way people do when a journey
brings them together. I walked for a while in company
with a town-planner from Groningen who was interested
in how, in such a horizontal world, everything seemed
high—the *wadlopers* and channel markers looked particularly tall above the mud. Van der Zee talked about
other *wadlopes* he had made. On one recent trip with
some soldiers, who were carrying full battle equipment,
he and an officer had been forced to carry one of the
exhausted men. It was generally agreed in our group
that it helped to be doing something like this for pleasure, and that perhaps there was an additional compensation in doing something most people would consider
nutty.

"Most people," for that matter, presently considered
as inevitable the reclamation of the Waddenzee; it was
in the Dutch blood, and after the completion of the
Delta project and the Lauwerszee works, the Waddenzee
was clearly next in line. Already there were demands

for a dam to carry a motorway from the mainland to Ameland, the island to the west of Schiermonnikoog, and if one dam, why not two? Then the area between could be drained and reclaimed. Van der Zee said that the current slogan of the reclaimers was recreation room rather than new farmland, and that they wanted to make the beaches and dunes of the islands "more accessible." However, opposition was being organized. A Groningen group was turning out pamphlets to convince people that the islands were better off as islands, that the Lauwerszee reclamation would create plenty of woods and fresh-water lakes for recreation, and that what was needed in Holland was the preservation of an area which was totally natural and even "difficult," like the Waddenzee. There would be no harm, of course, in making the mainland coast more accessible, and improving the facilities for salt-water swimming, sailing, and sport fishing. Van der Zee thought the message of the anti-reclaimers was getting across. A commission to study the future of the Waddenzee had been set up in The Hague, and that was a start.

We changed course several times, once at a gully, and again on reaching a bright orange marker buoy which lay with its chain and anchor exposed on the sand. About halfway across the Wad the thin rain lifted, and suddenly we could see the low sand dunes and square church tower of Schiermonnikoog. We crossed a second channel, the Schildknoopen, which had two feet of water in it, and thereafter the going was on firmer sand. In fact, it was now possible to lope, to take long, bouncy strides, but I found that a thick build-up of mud in the toes of my sneakers didn't make for comfortable loping. In the group ahead of us four or five young men began to sing—a somewhat tuneless indication of high morale which led a Randstad schoolteacher in our band to quote Tacitus, an early observer of these parts: *Frisiae non cantant* ("Frisians can't sing").

In the channel called Sprutel, the last of the fingers of the western arm reaching in around the island, the tide was flooding. Van der Zee noted this fact, not from any movement of water but from the trace of white scum on the edge of the channel. We crossed the Sprutel where it was barely damp, near the point where it buried itself in the broad watershed under the south shore of Schiermonnikoog. At two-thirty we climbed up onto the *kwelder* and a few minutes later we were up on the dike which runs around a small polder. We walked along to a pier, where later that evening the ferry boat came to take us back over the risen waters of the Wad, and now a welcome bus waited to carry the weary *wadlopers* into the island village cafés. There, in dry clothes, we drank hot soup and neat genever and felt the convivial camaraderie that results from arduous, peaceful exercise. We had each done something we felt slightly pleased about, and we had done it together.

PART THREE

The Country as a Community

"I care, You care, We care."

❧ 16 ❧

ONE NIGHT IN AMSTERDAM, with ten minutes on hand before the time set to call on some friends, I went into a small tavern called De Schouw, just off Overtoom, a street of lower-middle-class flats and unsuccessful-looking automotive supply shops, and, seated at the bar, found myself being addressed by the narrator of Camus's novel *The Fall*. "The more I accuse myself, the more I have a right to judge you. Even better, I provoke you into judging yourself." It was clear right away that this seedy domestic atmosphere of the area around Overtoom was better suited to the descent and collapse of what Camus called a "judge-penitent," a person who has to confess himself, than the locale Camus picked for his book, the red-light district of the Zeedijk and an exotic seamen's bar called Mexico City. But it also became clear to me, after the first shock of finding life so closely imitating art, that the man on the barstool next to me was not a Frenchman, like Jean-Baptiste Clamence in *The Fall*. Moreover, he was of a less melodramatic metaphysical turn of mind than that former Parisian lawyer. His self-accusation released the facts that he had had a Dutch father, a German mother, and had spent most of his life in Switzerland. He exposed rotten teeth in a wide grin as he confessed to being an alcoholic. His "problem," insofar as I was able to grasp it in ten minutes, was that Holland wasn't doing anything for him, or enough for him—he had come "home" from Switzerland expecting to be rescued, and no one was throwing him a lifebuoy. Could he have seen or grabbed a lifebuoy if one had been thrown? His last job had been with a Yugoslav airline, and those Serbs and Croats had done more for him than the Dutch. Though they had fired him, too. He said petulantly, as the bartender handed him a drink and then, on a chit, drew a fifth line through four pencil marks, that he wished he had stayed in Switzerland, or gone to America or India, where there was perhaps less help but more freedom. "Here," he said, "there are plenty of people to help you when you've fallen. But there's no one to catch you when you're just about to fall."

Accusing Holland, he provoked me to judge it. Although I made my excuses and left to keep the appointment I was glad at that point to have, the subject stayed in my mind. His diagnosis seemed in the first instance faulty: he was falling, not about to fall. And as I thought about it, it soon seemed to me that this friendless, alcoholic case was general rather than specifically Dutch; however, that being so, he couldn't have done much better than come home. Tight fit and crowded conditions hadn't made Dutchmen asocial—perhaps the reverse was true. Holland, in fact, had better arrangements than any other country I knew for letting people lead their own

lives, letting them be independent to a point where sometimes, in existential fashion, the freedom hurt, there was
so much of it—the way the hurt pressured Descartes
into complaining about it, and perhaps was hurting this
man too. And within this freedom existed a system for
caring for people whose lives were for one reason or another in disarray. Soon there were going to be attempts
to put this man together again. I suspected he knew this,
and it was the reason he was in a bar off the Overtoom
in Amsterdam, rather than in Zurich or San Francisco or
Bombay.

❦

If you wanted to find the apotheosis of all that being a
contemporary Dutchman is not, you would most likely
find it in the imaginative literature of the eighteenth
century; for example, in *Robinson Crusoe*. Crusoe is a
man without society, without community. He has no
crowds to bother him, no traffic problems, no population
explosion, no anxieties about government housing or the
need for recreation or the power-hungry state. He makes
his own house, plays his own games. More justly than
an absolute monarch he can say: *"L'état c'est moi."* I
discussed this subject with Dr. Arie Querido, Professor of Social Medicine at the University of Amsterdam. Addressing a recent conference on World Population and Mental Health, Dr. Querido described a pair of

Eskimos, living alone, who have a baby; noticing with horror that it has no teeth, they take it out to leave it in the snow to die. There they come across an old dying woman who tells them that the baby is normal: teeth will grow. Which makes the point that there is a level of social density below which "mutual support has become impossible, communication breaks down, and the transfer of knowledge, traditional and cultural lore is impeded." We need people.

The Dutch are at a far extreme from the Eskimos; they have a high social density. So high, in fact, that like a family in a crowded living room, where some are reading, some writing, some sewing, and some listening to the radio, while Papa broods, they have learned how to pretend at any given moment that some of the people— particularly those who can be lumped in a group—are invisible or are not there. It is a course of action the Dutch have taken since the sixteenth century, when the rebellion against Spanish rule underlined the religious disharmony of the so-called United Provinces. The Netherlands then contained many Catholics, as well as the Calvinists who were in the forefront of the struggle, and the country has continued to contain them—indeed, more and more of them. Holland also holds more moderate Protestants, whose zeal has been put into politics and commerce as well as religion, and it welcomes foreigners seeking sanctuary, such as Portuguese Jews, French Huguenots, and, in recent years, refugees from Indonesia. Both the Calvinists and Roman Catholics have insisted that education have a religious framework. Groups of farmers and political parties, like the Socialists, have made their own particular demands and formed their own identities. The result is a country which may at first seem comprehensively Dutch, through and through, but which will split open into half a dozen major fragments, each of which will in turn flake off into many parts. The Dutch word for this separateness within their society is *verzuiling*. *Zuilen* are pillars or columns, and *verzuiling* means the state of being in columns, or pillarization, each pillar "valuable in its own right," to quote Professor J. Goudsblom of the University of Amsterdam, "and together indispensable in supporting the national structure."

One breakdown of this condition would show three main columns: Catholic, Protestant, and "Liberal-Humanist." A further diagnosis would reveal over twenty political parties and eighty religious denominations and countless groups. There are five or six hundred different associations in the northeast polder alone—associations for playing football, listening to records, talking about farm problems. The example generally quoted by Dutch sociologists is the Roman Catholic Goat-breeders Association. Religion enters everywhere, and thus Holland not only has an International Red Cross but, to take care of various denominational intricacies, a Green Cross, White-Yellow Cross, and Orange-Green Cross. Although it makes little economic sense, some small northeast polder villages have three schools and three churches, all at a careful distance from one another. (A now-repealed 1853 law stipulated a distance of 420 feet,

which is 20 ells, between churches in order to preserve
the peace.) In Emmeloord, the central market town of
the northeast polder, there are twenty-six schools, which
mainly provide for various denominations. A polder
study points out that "a not inconsiderable part of the
working population of Emmeloord consists of teachers."
But Emmeloord is a new town, and thus quite hetero-
geneous. Many towns are not, and mentioning one by
name to a Dutchman, he is liable to say, "Oh yes, they
are very Calvinist there," or "That's an extremely Catholic place." Katwijk aan Zee, for instance, is notoriously
Calvinist, while the adjacent town of Katwijk aan Rijn is
Catholic. There are Catholic newspapers, Protestant
newspapers, and Socialist newspapers. (There have been,
however, no Sunday newspapers since the war and the
destruction of Dutch Jewry. There used to be a Jewish
paper printed in Amsterdam on Sundays and in that
country of avid newspaper readers it was popular with
more than Jews.) There are Catholic libraries and Protestant libraries. You can tell the difference between the
churches by looking at the steeples: the Catholics have a
cross, the Lutherans a swan, and the Reformed Calvinists
a weathercock. Before the Second World War it was cus-
tomary in Dutch Catholic homes to turn off the radio if a
Protestant preacher came on. One of the quickest ways
to embarrass a Dutchman who doesn't know you extremely well is to ask him for the times of Sunday
church services—if he is a Calvinist he won't know anything about the Catholics, and vice versa, and if he is
what the Dutch call "unchurchly"—which covers the

agnostics, atheists, free and dubious thinkers—he will be exceptionally anguished at being confronted with such a question at all.

In Holland like talks to like. This is true not only in terms of religion (and it is perhaps interesting that more of the Dutch approve of racially mixed marriages than approve of religiously mixed marriages), but in terms of occupation. Although there seems to be little class snobbery, perhaps because of the all-pervasive bourgeoisie and a lack of clear-cut classes, there is an abrupt lack of contact between a man who does one thing and a man who does another. There are pillars of experts, and great efforts have to be made to get, say, sociologists, engineers, and architects to discuss a common problem. Everything and everyone has a distinct place in the divine scheme. Titles and degrees are to be used if one doesn't want to offend professors, doctors, engineers, technicians, and maiden ladies.

Menno Brandsma, who works as a biologist in the new polders, told me how surprised he had been during the first year he had lived in the new town of Dronten. With limited facilities that had had to be shared, Catholic children had played with Calvinist in nursery schools and their parents had talked with each other; the condition of being pioneers had outweighed the problems of tradition. But as time passed and the population grew, and more farmers came to farm the new land, bringing their conservative ideas with them, Dronten became what Mr. Brandsma called "a mirror of Holland." Even so, he didn't expect this segmented state to last forever.

As the pillars rest on a foundation of common citizenship, language, environment, and heritage, so are they being continually bridged by common services and events. Elementary school imposes the same curriculum and the same discipline on all Dutch children from six to twelve. Disasters like war and flood have had their unifying effects on the Dutch, and cars and television every day weave an enclosing net. The television programing authorities are run by five associations (one Protestant, one Catholic, one Liberal, one Socialist, and one neutral—though even neutrality is considered a position in Holland), and there is a lot of sermonizing and sectarian speech-making. But there are also song festivals, football games, bad movies, the news, and the occasional humor or satire program on which a remark is made or a spectacle offered, like a nude girl, and twelve and a half million Dutch are bound in the accord of common shock. Car drivers are not furnished with Catholic cars or Protestant highways, and most of them belong to a nationwide organization, the A.N.W.B., which provides road signs, route maps, and a splendid free roadside breakdown service. There are, of course, no pillars in a traffic jam.

All in all, one might say that, in the maintenance of a densely settled community which wishes to remain harmonious, *verzuiling* plays a worthwhile part. The pillars create a nondestructive spirit of competition. They encourage ardor and remove apathy. Because they are so various, they prevent lines being sharply drawn between one side and another: it takes two to make a fight, and when you have twenty-two you have instead, at the most, a constant quarrel.

❧ 17 ❧

To some Dutchmen the religious preoccupations of their fellow countrymen are a kind of hangover. "The Dutch are victims of a sixteenth-century mental state," says the chess grand master Jan Hein Donner; and he thinks that Calvinism is to blame—it robs man of his self-respect. In towns and sections of the countryside which are largely Calvinist, there is what Willem Banning of Leiden University calls "a deeper awareness of the wickedness and depravity of the human race." Barneveld, a stanchly Calvinist town in the Veluwe, can be counted on to provide illustrative material in this respect several times a year, having a dominie who condemns parishioners for riding bicycles on Sundays and denounces a young couple in his flock for the "grave sin" of purchasing a television set. In Staphorst, a little further north, the television sets are secretly installed at night—according to unchurchly rumor—though in Staphorst modern times have been openly accepted in the shape of land-reparceling schemes, and several souvenir shops cater for tourists who come to the village to stare at the hidebound Staphorsters in their quaint old-fashioned costumes. Yet tourist cameras are still now and then smashed in Staphorst on Sundays, and suspected adulterers are paraded around the village on farmcarts and then banished from the place. Hex signs are painted outside the houses. Vacant-looking children with squints and other deformities show the inbred signs of the enclosed nature of the village, and outsiders believe, whatever the facts, that no Staphorst girl gets married until she is pregnant; and they point out the low bedroom windows through which young men are encouraged to climb.

But this is perhaps the most highly colored aspect of the matter. "Things could not have been produced by God in any other manner or order than that in which they were produced," said Spinoza, and the fact is that God is in the air in Holland—religion is taken with a seriousness that doesn't seem to exist in many other so-called Christian countries. Even the unchurchly, the *buitenkerkelijke*, make sure that you understand that their being outside an institutional church has nothing to do with lacking a religious temperament. The most doctrinaire and conservative Calvinists now make up less than 10 per cent of the population, and some 28 per cent are Protestants of a less strict Reformed persuasion—though they may still go to church twice on Sundays. All Sunday long in the village of Surhuisterveen, where I lived for a while, on the Friesland-Groningen border, the sound of hymn-singing came over the back gardens, either from the churches or from houses to which

people had returned from church, still singing. In few of
these houses would people imagine starting a meal without saying grace; in many, a reading from the Bible
would take place afterward. A cross will be on the wall
behind the television set, and on a side table a pile of
religious magazines and missionary material for which
donations have been given. The young may not be quite
so flamboyantly earnest about religion, but I got the impression from Enneus Heerma, a political science student
in Amsterdam who continues to say grace and go to
church, and who also watches television and rides a bike
on Sundays, that the Deity was a real dimension in his
life.

As the Spanish found during their occupation of the
Low Countries, the natives of the region have always
been so inclined. Life goes on in the paintings of
Breughel, the harvest is gathered and the feast cele-
brated, but in the corners of the fields and along the
roadsides there are crosses and gibbets on which people
are hung, for their faith. There is the saying, "One
Dutchman a theologian, two Dutchmen a sect, three
Dutchmen a schism." But in recent years the reputation for theological speculation and controversy has
shifted from the Reformed to the Dutch Catholics, who
number roughly five million—some 40 per cent of the
population. This is not to say that these are all religious radicals. A study made in the 1950's of the bulb-
growing town of Sassenheim indicated that Catholics
there felt even more strongly opposed than the stanch
Calvinists to "mixed marriages." As recently as 1954

the Dutch Catholic bishops sent out a pastoral letter forbidding their flocks to join Socialist trade unions,
visit Socialist meetings, read Socialist newspapers, or listen to Socialist radio programs, lest they be excluded
from the sacraments. But by 1966, 15 per cent of all marriages involving a Catholic were mixed; in towns with
more than 100,000 people the figure was 30 per cent. The
countryside has been becoming urbanized, and the Dutch
Catholic hierarchy has reflected the intense socially
aware climate of Randstad Holland. A Dutchman, Adrian
VI, was the last non-Italian pope (in the sixteenth century), and when during the Second Vatican Council in
1962 Dutch Cardinal Alfrink interrupted a speech by the
conservative Italian Cardinal Ottaviani, after he had
exceeded his time-limit, it was regarded by many as a gesture—perhaps typically Dutch in its tactlessness—of the
contemporary urban forces of renewal in the church in
opposition to the Roman forces of inertia. Despite the
ban of 1954 against Socialist ties, in 1966 a Dutch priest,
Nico van Hees, was working as a reporter for the Socialist paper *Het Vrije Volk.*

The leader of the Dutch Catholic *risorgimento,* until he
died in 1966, was Bishop Wilhelmus Bekkers, who
(writes van Hees) did "for Dutch Catholics what Pope
John did for the world church." On television Bishop
Bekkers told viewers that birth control was a matter of
individual conscience. "Although he wasn't a learned
theologian, he inspired new theological thought," a
Dutch Catholic told me. "He tried to loosen up the
atmosphere surrounding mixed marriages. He had a vi-

sion of one Christian church which he managed to get across—sometimes he told Catholics that the Lutherans had done more to develop the truth of Christianity. He attempted to relieve the pressure of sin which old-fashioned Catholic theology imposes on married couples trying to avoid having more children. In Rome he was critical of some of the more rarefied aspects of the Council." (A note: Some 60 per cent of Dutch Catholic women practice contraception. It may be germane that the company now making roughly 14 per cent of the total world production of the Pill is the Dutch firm, Organon—"our lobby in the Vatican," as one Catholic engineer called it while discussing his church with me.) Bishop Bekkers encouraged those who were questioning the need for clerical celibacy, promoting communal meals called agape feasts which are shared by Catholic and non-Catholic, reforming the liturgy of the Mass, and promoting lay participation in diocesan councils and even in the nomination of new bishops.

The fervor has been widespread, with more than twelve thousand lay discussion groups and numerous clerical conferences at which theologians have speculated with refreshing candor about such subjects as original sin, virgin birth, and the resurrection of Jesus. The speculation is present in the new Dutch catechism, a more than six-hundred-page work which has sold over four hundred thousand copies in Holland. The catechism charitably fails to give firm doctrinal answers to the old catechetical questions, such as "Who made us?" Instead, treating human and divine issues as necessarily fraught with ambiguity, it discusses Hindu belief, Marxism, the Reformation, and homosexuality; on the latter, for example: "It is not the fault of the individual if he or she is not attracted to the other sex. . . . The very sharp strictures of Scripture on homosexual practices (Genesis 29; Romans 1) must be read in context. Their aim is not to pillory the fact that some people experience this perversion inculpably. They denounce a homosexuality which had become the prevalent fashion and had spread to many who were really quite capable of normal sexual sentiments." On the subject of God, the new catechism talks more in the accents of Thomas à Kempis than Thomas Aquinas: "God is free of the world, but He is still at the depths of its being. . . . The assertion of His distance and presence at once gives revelation the very tension, grandeur and impact through which man feels that God is speaking. Our heart expands in the unfathomable mystery which lies outside the paths of our thought."

In many churches—where attendance at mass is higher than in other, nominally "Catholic" countries—plaster saints have been cleared out. Private confession is no longer much practiced, partly because most people are no longer bothered by the sexual "sins" which comprised so much of the material to be confessed. Public penitential services are held before Christmas and Easter. Experiments are also being made in monastic life. The Dominican Edward Schillebeeckx, who is regarded in conservative circles in Rome as one of the chief Dutch troublemakers, writes: "It is no longer a matter of minor changes. For a monastic institution that cannot or will not adapt itself, there is nothing left but to face the consequences and organize its collective funeral." In Eindhoven three Trappist monks left the contemplative silence of the cloister to live in an ordinary house and work in a hospital, a school, and a laboratory, wearing normal clothes, going to the movies, and smoking their cigars and pipes. In Amsterdam three Capuchins have gone to live in a flat; one visits the sick and aged in the neighborhood, while the second works in a metal factory, and the third is a gardener in the Amsterdamse Bos. In other cities, other monks are making similar efforts, alone or in groups, to fit what was originally a medieval conception to the exigencies of contemporary life.

Where the sting of progress in the church is really felt is in regard to the rules on priestly celibacy. In 1967, 115 priests left the church; between 1965 and 1969 the total number of priests in Holland dropped by 400; the number of ordinations went down from 421 in 1957 to 145 in 1969. An inquiry made among 180 ex-priests showed that nearly half of them had married within two years, and that most of them would go back into the church if the celibacy rule were changed. Father Walter Goddijn, the secretary of the Dutch Pastoral Council, has called papal policy in this respect that of an ostrich, while the board of the Catholic students union has issued a statement saying, "A primate who cannot think on higher levels than that of Italian sexual morality stops functioning for us." Ninety-seven per cent of the Catholic students in Amsterdam have supported one of their chaplains, Father Jos Vrijburg, in his request for permission to continue his work as a priest after he is married; he has announced his engagement. An eighty-strong group of priests recently met in Amsterdam and appealed to their bishops to set up certain sections of the country where married priests could work. It is, after all, the country where home and family count. At the end of 1969 the eight Dutch bishops endorsed the resolution of the pastoral council opposing mandatory celibacy.

Other countries, particularly England and America, have shown a friendly interest in the Dutch situation, which gives them a strong taste of the future. Paul Johnson, the Catholic editor of the *New Statesman*, has written, "I should like to see the Vatican abolished and headquarters moved to a country (Holland, for instance) where there is a better climate for discussion." Two Dutch laymen, Michel van der Plas and Henk Suèr, describing things, say: "The situation is a source of joy." This has not been the reaction in Rome. There, Holland has a reputation of being a problem child: it has been rude to the Inquisition, to the Duke of Alba, and to Philip II of Spain. Several recent encyclicals have appeared to be aimed directly at Dutch notions about the Eucharist (*Mysterium fidei*) and about a priest's obligation to remain unmarried (*Sacerdotalis caelibatus*). And though the recently appointed pro-Prefect of the Congregation of Studies in Rome, Monsignor Garonne, has said that no one should judge the Dutch too quickly or superficially, the Dutch themselves have had the impression that that is the way they have been judged in Rome. Cardinal Ottaviani, as secretary to the Roman Congregation of Doctrine, declared that the Dutch Pastoral Council (convened in November 1966 to study clerical celibacy, among other anxieties), didn't deserve such a name, and that there was no precedent in canon law for this Dutch form of internal deliberation. Other Roman theologians have seemed to be bothered by the Dutch disinterest in discussing heaven, hell, or the sex of angels. Pope Paul himself wrote to the Dutch hierarchy praising them for convening the Pastoral Council, but he took the opportunity (having created the opportunity) to say that they should be prudent and on the watch for rash and erroneous opinions.

Many Dutch Catholics believe that they, with their horror of secrecy, are simply talking about matters that other Catholics, including Catholics in Rome, are talking about in whispers. They do not want to sound schismatic. There was a time when three thousand Dutchmen volunteered for the Papal army to defend Pio Nono against Garibaldi, and today more than five thousand Dutch priests are working as Catholic missionaries in various parts of the world. But they believe that the spirit of absolutism which seems to emanate from the Roman Curia is a danger to the church. As the world gets more complex and more crowded and many things grow gigantic, so there has to be a constant effort to make things small, to give them a coherence of their own on a smaller scale that they may have some relevance to human life. The Dutch thus trust in a local church, responsive to the needs of a given place at a given time, relevant to an individual in Holland rather than to a historic concept in Rome. Hence much of their joy, which springs from a sense of freedom, of being individual. "Insofar as I am concerned personally," writes Father Schillebeeckx, "life in Holland forces me to take myself seriously, a state which I would not have reached outside Holland or simply by myself."

❧ 18 ❧

LIFE IS SERIOUS IN HOLLAND. It is a feature that hasn't always appealed to the refugees, exiles, and foreign-born who have come to make their home in the Lowlands. Indeed, there are moments in Holland when the stranger feels he has danced or sung for the last time. He begins to act twenty years older, and thinks cynically that one reason the Dutch are so good at looking after people is that they have so many to look after; that to care for those who need it is therapeutic for those who do the caring. And yet (and it is a big "and yet") the fact that the Dutch take the responsibilities of life so seriously may account for the very presence of these refugees and exiles. A Dutchman may not invite you to dinner in his own home, but he has always been hospitable with his crowded little country. Tolerance is perhaps an urban

virtue, more possible in cities than in rural places; and
although the Dutch haven't consistently been tolerant to
other Dutchmen (Grotius imprisoned, the nineteenth-
century mathematician Thomas Stieltjes allowed to live
impoverished in Toulouse, Spinoza declared an outcast
by the Amsterdam Jewish community, the filmmaker
Joris Ivens living in Paris because he feels officially unwelcome in Holland), it has been a refuge for some of the
greatest men: Descartes and Scaliger, Freud and Einstein. Madame Montessori, the teacher, came to live and
die in Holland. Frederick of Bohemia, deposed in 1619,
sought refuge in Holland and so did Kaiser Wilhelm
on the collapse of Germany in 1918. Leiden and other
universities attracted students from other countries.
Scotsmen like James Boswell came to Utrecht, and many
French to Leiden and Franeker. In 1685 a Frenchman
reckoned that half the total population with permanent
abodes in the province of Holland were foreigners or their
immediate descendants. The civil wars which went on in
France, Germany, and England during the seventeenth
century served to increase, as Sir William Temple
pointed out, "the swarm in this Country, not only by such
as were persecuted at home, but great numbers of peace-
able men, who came here to seek for quiet in their
Lives, and safety in their Possessions or Trades; like
those Birds that upon the approach of a rough Winter-
season, leave the Countrys where they were born and
bred, flye away to some kinder and softer Climate,
and never return till the Frosts are past, and the Winds
are laid at home." In Holland in the seventeenth cen-

tury, as in America during the nineteenth and twentieth centuries, it was possible to arrive poor and make a fortune. Jacob Poppen came penniless from Holstein to Amsterdam and died in 1624 a burgomaster and a millionaire. African slaves were free the moment they touched Dutch soil. The Pilgrim Fathers found a friendly refuge in Leiden. Flemish and Walloon refugees revived the weaving trade of that city and the cloth-bleaching industry of Haarlem. Antwerp provided craftsmen and merchants who invigorated Amsterdam. French Huguenots opened schools, introduced new methods in clock-making, taught the violin and culinary arts, and complained about the climate, the Dutch temperament, and the impossibility of learning such a language. (According to the French writer Bernard Pingaud there is still a French Jansenist Old Catholic church in Utrecht, "whose Bishop is regularly excommunicated by the Pope.") Portuguese and Spanish Sephardim came in great numbers at the end of the sixteenth century and prospered. Opposite the Montelbaan toren they built a copy of Solomon's temple—a galleried, triple-naved synagogue which every Saturday was crowded with five or six thousand worshippers. (However, they didn't dominate trade. Paul Zumthor writes that among Amsterdam's fifteen hundred biggest taxpayers in 1631, only six were Jews.)

Today in Holland the Dutch feel in many ways European. On television they see Bobby Charlton kicking off for England against Yugoslavia in Milan, and Miriam Mireille singing from Paris. Albert Heijn, the big supermarket chain, sells Hungarian jams and Spanish wine.

Beat groups sing in English, and Rotterdam, like New York and Osaka, is building a World Trade Center. In fact, although foreign experts like Professor Parkinson judge them the best-run nation in the world, the Dutch as Dutch feel politically insignificant—"a rapidly fading square inch between America and Russia," says the Dutch concert singer Tabe Bas—and they worry, in reverse proportion to their lack of control, about Nigeria, Czechoslovakia, Vietnam, and as always, the Bomb. But as a small country, Holland at least lacks the effects of great size and power that make for insularity. The Dutch feel close to other small countries, like Israel. Young people belong to organizations for European unity (Dutch cars often carry plates saying not only NL for Netherlands but EU for Europe Unie). Foreign Minister Luns uses his best influence to counter the French and get Britain admitted to the Common Market.

Within the Common Market, labor has a new freedom to cross national boundaries, but in Holland, with a shortage of nonskilled workers, many others enter as well. There are presently 12,000 Moroccans, 10,000 Turks, 10,000 Spaniards, 9,000 Italians, 1,500 Greeks, 1,000 Portuguese, and 1,000 Yugoslavs. Those are the legal immigrants, but many North Africans come in clandestinely, live in attics, and now and then cause a stink by slaughtering a sheep for a feast. Many Englishmen work in Dutch publishing and broadcasting, Australians fly for KLM, and Americans run stockbrokerage offices in the Weesperstraat or live creatively on barges along the Amstel. Dutch companies like Philips, with notable research departments, seek out bright graduates from universities in Switzerland, Spain, and Italy. Since 1601, in fact, the number of immigrants has exceeded the number of emigrants. To foreign nationals may be added some ten thousand Surinamers, Creole people from the former Dutch South American colony, and three hundred thousand refugees and repatriates from Indonesia who arrived between 1945 and 1964.

Twenty-five years after 1945, it is possible to forget how important the Indies used to be in the Dutch economy, and how ubiquitous was the Dutch image of themselves as imperial merchants. By the mid-nineteenth century the country's chief source of wealth was colonial trade. Reading Couperus's *Old People* one gets the impression that in The Hague *everyone* who counts is living off a connection with the Indies. In his book *Indonesia,* Bruce Grant writes: "At its prewar trading peak, the archipelago provided an income directly or indirectly to one in every seven Dutchmen." Before World War II the Dutch East Indies supplied some 90 per cent of the world's quinine, 86 per cent of its pepper, 37 per cent of its rubber, 19 per cent of its tea, and 17 per cent of its tin, as well as sugar, coffee, oil, and most of the world production of cigar wrappers. The profits from this trade fattened not only the Dutch merchant class but also the self-esteem of the burghers; their damp little homeland was the seat of a great warm colonial empire. And while the Dutch themselves may have made little impression on Indonesia—beyond running it efficiently, throwing the most intelligent radical Indonesians into detention camps, making a great deal of money, and drinking a lot of gin—Indonesia itself had a pronounced effect on them. The old Dutch Calvinist skin softened in the tropics. The spices got to them. Intermarriage was common.

Today, the Dutch seem well rid of their colonial burden. They have been able to throw off some of the old "regents' mentality" that went with it. It has done them good to lose a little of that burgher fat. The loss of their captive export market brought about, after the Second World War, a deliberate government policy of managing the economy, keeping prices and wages low, and promoting industrial expansion. The policy has been exceptionally successful. But however fortunate the loss of empire has been in retrospect, at the time it was a crisis. The Dutch met the emergency as they would a flood, with well-organized energy and a humanity they hadn't been so noted for in the Indies. The return and immigration were handled with skill and tact. The Indonesians included some pure Dutch, some mixed blood, and some pure Indonesian. Many Christian, highly educated islanders from Ambon, in the Moluccas, decided to leave their home and come to Holland after Indonesian independence. Two hundred thousand Indonesian residents came to Holland between 1945 and 1949, and although the country was still in a bad way from the German occupation, a great deal was done for them. In Jakarta the emigrants were interviewed. Details of age, family size, education, occupation, and relatives or friends in Holland were sent ahead. When the refugee ships arrived, they were met by committees which arranged for temporary accommodation (paid for by the government) in various towns and villages so that the Indonesians weren't bunched in one ghettolike spot. Medical examinations were given, and treatment and hospitalization for those who needed it. Each immigrant was given a year's free supply of clothing and help in finding a job. Room was found in boarding schools for children who came without their parents. In the years from 1950 to 1964 the equivalent of fifteen million dollars was granted to the immigrants for clothes, furniture, housing, and allowances to keep them until they were employed. In 1957 Indonesia threw out a batch of people as undesirable aliens, and when they arrived Queen Juliana spent a night in their hostel with them. Twenty-two homes have been established for old Indonesians, and in them the elderly women can wear their sarongs and kabojes, and sit down several times a week to a *rijsttafel*.

Many of these refugees have retained their Easternness. The Ambonese elders have clustered together and will never be assimilated, though their children have been happily absorbed in Dutch schools. A few of the young Indonesians wonder how they can retain the best of their heritage while making a career in the West. I talked with one very intelligent young Indonesian who works for the government in The Hague, and he said that though the climate and the stolid Dutch temperament annoyed him, he greatly appreciated the blessings of Dutch civilization, particularly "the relative anonymity within a coherent community. In Indonesia where

there are fifty-two languages—and arguments to be had
in all of them—we lived with wide-open windows: there
was no privacy. Here, most of all there is relative well-
being and peacefulness."

In some ways Dutch tolerance is skin-deep, but the
skin powerfully shapes it. The average Dutchman does
not want his daughter to go out with a Surinamer, and
he believes that Moroccans are dirty, Turks dangerous,
and the Indonesians slothful and noisy. Despite this, he
finds himself committed to a belief in equality and
fraternity among people of different beliefs and backgrounds. Although he won't invite an Indonesian home
to dinner, he wouldn't invite an Englishman or a fellow
Dutchman either, unless the latter happened to do exactly what he did and had the same religion and family
status. He is, however, happy to accept Indonesians as
colleagues, to eat Indonesian food, and attend such functions as the annual Indo-Dutch fair in The Hague. Many
of the top posts in the armed forces are held by ex-
officers from the Indies. Perhaps the most influential
factor among ordinary people is the food, for in the
Dutch equivalent of a hotdog stand, the *Automatiek* or
Patates Frites shop, you can buy such cheap, spicy
Indonesian foods as *nasi* balls and *loempia*, which is a
kind of giant egg roll. And youth is the other thing. If
you stand in the open doorway of a *Patates Frites* shop
in central Amsterdam, munching a hot *loempia* and
watching people pass, you will see among them Indonesians of all shades of skin, from light to dark, some alone,
some together, and many who are young with white

companions—boys and girls, young men and women. To someone from England or America the commonness of the sight seems at first a striking thing. But pretty soon the naturalness of it is a nice relief; one doesn't need to have, and soon one simply doesn't have, a reaction.

Some Saturday afternoons while we were in Katwijk I took my oldest daughter to a stable in Voorschoten, an elegant establishment where well-groomed children rode around a ring on well-groomed horses and learned the elements of equestrian etiquette from a very stern Dutch woman. Several of the children were Indonesian. I occasionally stood watching alongside their father, a very distinguished-looking gentleman, and would exchange with him a few words on the weather or the difficulty of keeping up with the demands of children for riding crops and riding boots. His children were wearing (as was my daughter) black rubber rather than brown leather boots. They had no need, springing from lack of confidence, to dress for appearances. And one day in Lunteren I stood waiting to use the one public telephone in the main street while a very pretty Indonesian girl chattered away, slipping in a *dubbeltje* or a *quartje* every time the meter showed her time was almost up. I was joined in my wait by a plump, middle-aged Dutchman. Soon he was more impatient than I, and began discussing where the next telephone was to be found at the station. He prowled around the booth, giving the girl meaningful looks and muttering to himself. Finally she hung up, collected her purse, and stepped out, ignoring us. The Dutchman turned to me and said, "Teenagers!"

❦

If the Dutch have an object for open intolerance, it is the Germans. A slight gap between the generations exists in this respect, and one should perhaps exclude those Dutch born after 1945, who do not often understand their elders' bitterness. There are, however, plenty of Dutch stories to illustrate the preoccupation with the neighbor to the east. Many people talk of answering a knock at the door and finding a German there who says, "I would like to bring in my wife and show her the house. I lived here during the war." One man who owns a windmill converted into a summer house denied (in a white-hot rage) the request of a German to come in and take photographs. The windmill-owner's son told his father he was wrong to act in this way. The man asked the boy what he would have done. The boy said: "I would have told them they could take photographs and what the charge was." In the west of Holland people ask, "Have you heard about the Germans and their beach bunkers?" and proceed to explain how German tourists dig big pits on the beach, walled with sand ramparts to keep the wind out, and decorated with German flags and signs saying "BESETZT," which means, of all things, "OC-CUPIED." They then lie in these pits and bake like corpulent lobsters, returning to the same spot daily throughout their vacation, treating the pit as their private property. The Dutch laugh, uneasily, at this behavior.

In the seaside towns in summer, as in the bulb region during the spring, three-quarters of the visitors appear to be German. Most Dutch people drive German cars, but the many German-owned cars can be distinguished by their white-background license plates and often by an optional D-for-Deutschland plate. One begins to have an irrational sympathetic response to those Germans who do not drive a Volkswagen, Opel, or Mercedes—who have a Fiat or a Peugeot instead, or tow an English sailing boat. (In Friesland I saw a German car towing a little sloop called *Emma Peel*, the name of the heroine of the British television thriller series *The Avengers*, which is very popular in Germany.) But in Katwijk and the west most people act like the windmill-owner's son: they accept the Germans and charge them for the privilege. The Ruhr's eight million are unavoidably there, next door, and West Germany's staggered holidays have been so misarranged from the Dutch point of view that the Ruhr is on holiday during July, when most of Holland is. Outside this short, overburdened season there are signs in the windows of every other house in the beach-front towns—occasionally in Dutch, *Kamer met ontbijt,* but more often in German, *Zimmer mit Frühstuck.* For the German invasion the Dutch move into their tents and caravans and basements, and go into paroxysms of spring cleaning to make their rooms, flats, and houses ready. Then they rub their hands at all the Deutschmarks and giggle at the fat-thighed German women in their stretch pants, and the men in big sunglasses, taking the fresh air and coastal sunshine. It is a tricky situation. As the Duke de Baena points out: "Twenty years ago, thanks to the Germans, the Dutch were eating their cheap tulip bulbs [note: not the expensive bulbs] in order to survive; to-day, the closest friends and lovers of the tulip are the Germans."

It is a situation in which there are rare instances of tact. In an Amsterdam *rondvaartboot*, or canal sightsee-ing boat, the guide talks in four languages, and passing the house where Anne Frank lived he says explicitly in Dutch, French, and English that this is where the Frank family hid from the Gestapo during the war. In German all he says is, "This is the house of the family Frank." What really annoys the Dutch is when some German says, *"Nicht gewusst"* ("I didn't know . . ."). They have heard it too often. They have heard it from Claus von Amsberg, who said it thoughtlessly and perhaps sincerely when he was being questioned about being a Hitler Youth, before marrying Princess Beatrix. And what annoys people from other countries is finding that the Dutch can act like Germans, perhaps as a result of being landlords to the annual invasion: master racism rubs off. The danger is recognized. "We see ourselves in the Ger-mans," said Mr. de Lange, a sound engineer, "that's why we dislike them." And when I found myself talking to Mr. van Soest, an official of The Hague water supply, not about water but about the deportation of the Jews, he said that it was the worst thing that had ever happened in Holland—"Not just for what it showed about the Ger-mans, but for what it told us about ourselves, about man." One hundred and forty thousand Jews lived in

Holland before the war. One hundred and ten thousand were deported and of them all but five thousand died in the camps and gas chambers. Some eight thousand survived in Holland by going into hiding. A few of the Dutch still ask themselves what they, the Dutch, did or did not do.

The Dutch were caught in many ways unprepared by the Second World War. They first tried to remain neutral, as they had successfully done in the First World War. Then, invaded, they fought hard for five days and capitulated in confusion, with the Queen and government fleeing to England, and the Germans bombing Rotterdam. Historians now say that there may be some excuse in the faulty communications between German field and air commanders, and that there was a failure to convey to the bombers the progress of surrender talks. In any event, Holland surrendered on the afternoon of May 14, 1940; that morning, after planes first bombed the Rotterdam water supply, German incendiaries were dropped on the city: 900 people were killed and 78,500 were made homeless.

For a while the Germans gave the impression that they were trying to bring Holland into the Third Reich. The Dutch were close kin, good Aryan stock, so why not National Socialize them? However, German police rule was soon in force: everyone over fifteen had to carry a *persoonsbewijs*—an identity card which, in the case of Jews, also had a J stamped on it. Queen Wilhelmina (whom Churchill once, with knowing humor, called the greatest man he knew) made occasional broadcasts from London, and Radio Orange came from the BBC for fif-

teen minutes daily. In 1943 the Germans confiscated all
the radio sets they could lay their hands on. For a while
Hitler and Himmler apparently toyed with the idea of
deporting the entire Dutch nation to the east, but when
deportation began, in July 1942, those who went were
the Jews.

Today there are Jews who complain that the Dutch
did little for them at that time. Some of the younger
generation of Dutch seem to pretend that there is a
myth of heroic resistance to the Germans, just so that
they can say it wasn't so. In fact, resistance and help for
the Jews was neither widespread nor generally heroic,
but here and there it existed; and the heres and theres
are important. The people in any country who are ready
to defy a ruthless occupation force are always going to
be few. Most of the Dutch Jews like the Jews elsewhere
cooperated with the Germans in all the bureaucracy of
registration, segregation, and the administration of holding camps in Holland. They were encouraged in their
doom by being given jobs and power over one another.
There were lists of so-called "exempt" people which encouraged compliance rather than escape. Like most of
the Dutch, most of the Dutch Jews went along with
German orders, hoping to stay out of trouble until the
very end, hoping and living with all the illusions they
could muster. A few fought back. In early 1941 bands of
young Jews in Amsterdam beat up some Dutch Nazis
and killed one. But an ostrichlike attitude was more
prevalent. In London the Dutch government in exile
refused to acknowledge what was actually happening.
In Holland public officials did little to arouse opposition

to the Germans, and most people tried to avert their eyes. "We saw the Jews being taken away and did nothing," one man said to me; he still feels the anguish of it. Another writes: "One felt sorry for the Jews and congratulated oneself on not being one of them. People gradually got used to Jews having the worst of it." *Het Parool*, the underground paper, wrote at the time, "Many of our people are undisturbed. . . . They are blind to the criminal acts by which part of our Dutch population in our own, hitherto safe country is gradually being forced to live like hunted animals, without any protection from the law, fearing for their lives." Officials maintained as usual their immaculate records. The trains, even the trains to Belsen and Auschwitz, ran uninterrupted through Holland. The only inefficiency was unhelpful: the Dutch Red Cross, alone among international Red Cross services, seemed unable to get parcels through to Dutch prisoners in Germany.

Some took a stand against the Germans—among them, the officials of Dutch churches who courageously signed their names to a letter opposing German plans to sterilize the Jews in May 1943. R. P. Cleveringa, a professor at Leiden University, made a speech denouncing the dismissal of two Jewish colleagues, and students at Leiden and Delft went on strike for the same cause. In February 1941 the Amsterdam dockworkers quit work to oppose the first registration of the Jews, and this led to a more general strike. And though a few Dutchmen played Judas and turned the Jews in to the authorities, many helped the Jews who had the courage and good sense to go into hiding.

Two or three hundred thousand Dutchmen of all denominations went underground during the war. They were known as *fietsers* (*cyclists*) or *onderduikers* (divers), and two clandestine national organizations worked to help them. One of these organizations had fifteen thousand members, most of the early ones being devout Calvinists who, after their first fatalistic impulse to believe that God had sent the Germans to punish them, came round to the belief that the Germans were anti-Christ. Having thus squared their consciences for the sin of rebellion, they became hard-core fighters against the Nazi agents of Satanism. They distributed ration books to those in hiding and put a stop to profiteering when they could; for example, when the Volendam fishermen began to run a black-market in fish, prices were quickly brought back to normal by sinking a few of their boats. The *onderduiker* aid organizations were slow to begin with to help adult Jews, but they did a great deal for Jewish infants and children, finding foster homes for them. And as the adult Jews took the risks of going underground, so did many Dutch families take the risk of hiding them. Some did it spontaneously; some after much soul-searching. Often the poor acted sooner than the rich. The dangers were not small, and there were informers, even among the Jews. Often it was the Jews in a small town, who were well-known there, who went into hiding. Most of the Amsterdam Jews, who had few Gentile acquaintances, surrendered to false hopes, listening to the advice of the Jewish Council and in the end "going east" rather than into hiding.

It was a rabbitlike existence for most who went underground. "They did a lot of reading," I was told by a teacher whose family hid a group of Jews from late 1942 until the Germans departed; this family also hid four RAF men for five weeks until an escape route was organized for them. There were problems of diet, sanitation, health, and death. Some kept under cover in cellars and closets while others walked around with their host's identity cards. One Jew, who went into hiding with a family which was already sheltering other Jews, arrived from Rotterdam with a moving van containing many packing cases and his piano. It was a time in which people realized the drawbacks of a country with no real wilderness. Man had to devise his own ingenious nests in cupboards, attics, and root-cellars. In Hoorn a lady nicknamed Tante Dieuw, who lived in a house occupied by the German town commandant, hid eight Jews until they could be moved to a safer place. One farmer harbored a whole band of Jews. The Germans raided the place, searched it for five hours, and threatened to burn it down unless the Jews they knew were hiding there were handed over to them by the following day. "When the Jews decided to leave that night," writes Dr. Jacob Presser, the historian of Dutch Jewry during this time, "their host refused to let them go, saying: 'God is with us today and he will not desert us tomorrow.' And indeed every one of these Jews survived the war."

Friesland with its lakes, swamps, and wide meadows had some advantages of inaccessibility. One of Mr. Heerma's neighbors was given a farm in the new polder as recognition for his heroism in sheltering over fifty

Jews in Oldeboorn during the war. He had been caught. Shipped off to a concentration camp, he was injected with TB and made to wear a death's-head badge, which meant that he could be picked out at any time for summary execution—a proceeding generally conducted in his camp with thirty prisoners being ordered to hang thirty of their fellow captives. Enneus Heerma, to whom at twenty-four all this is history, said: "He is not in good shape now, this man. He drinks a lot. Now and then he goes into town and gets into a fight with a German tourist."

❦ 19 ❦

THE WAR HAS BEEN OVER twenty-five years, a generation, but its effects in Holland are to be seen. The Amsterdam diamond trade is not what it was. The Jewish quarter of that city, whose empty houses were devastated by firewood hunters during the hunger winter of 1944–5, still looks blitzed and empty, a site for development schemes that haven't matured; it now seems more suitable for road expansion and subway construction. One slightly less tangible effect of the war, some observers feel, has been an intensification of what was already a strong characteristic of the Dutch—their sense of care. Sir William Temple noted in the seventeenth century: "Charity seems to be very national among them." If Sir William was acquainted with the great Amsterdam surgeon Nicholas Tulp, one of whose anatomy lessons Rembrandt painted, he might have been aware of the doctor's motto: "In serving I consume myself." But whereas in former times Dutch charity and responsibility seemed focused on family, community, or co-religionists, it now has a wider reach. War guilt or a training in courage may be causes, and so may a denser, more urban society, which creates pressures that can be worked off in a concern for such remote events as Negro rights, the Israeli-Arab conflict, or Indian famines. Certainly victims of wars and floods and earthquakes these days find a full and quick response in Holland. After the 1953 floods, a nationwide appeal produced 100 million guilders in six months, which fully compensated the flood victims for the possessions they had lost, including their yachts, pianos, and paintings. After the Skopje earthquake in Yugoslavia there was an immediate and successful Dutch appeal for relief funds. In Calvinist Katwijk in one night local women collected forty thousand guilders for Israel. On Dutch television there is always some cause being pushed, which needs money and help, and the Dutch do not seem to tire of giving. In September 1965, Foreign Minister Luns got the government to make available a hundred thousand guilders to the Dutch section of the South African Defence and Aid fund, to finance legal assistance for persons accused of violating the apartheid laws, and the Dutch people collected a matching hundred thousand through auctions of art works and manuscripts, donations of book royalties, and private contributions. Nor do they only give money. Dutch engineers have worked out a method, adopted by the Egyptians, for saving the water-threatened temples at Philae. Dutch doctors work in war-shattered Nigeria. The city of New York, shattered by other things and needing assistance in the treatment of alcoholics, has got a Dutch specialist, Dr. Henry Krauweel, to commute regularly from Amsterdam to Manhattan to help. Within Holland—where Hals, Vermeer, and Rembrandt all died penniless—artists are now given grants from a fund made up of 1 per cent of the cost of building projects, while serious magazines receive government subsidies to help pay writers.

Although a system where help is so communal and so general might be expected to discourage perhaps the assistance of one man in one place, my own experience was that this isn't so. To take a perfectly homely example, I was painting the roof rack of my car with aluminum paint one afternoon in Lunteren, when a gust of wind blew under the sheet of newspaper, on top of the car, on which the paint can stood. The can tipped over. Aluminum paint ran in a wide deluge down the back of the car. I was floundering around rather unsuccessfully with turpentine soaked rags and paper towels, trying to adjust my car-owner's pride to the idea of a silver-grey streaked tailgate, when the lady next door appeared and without a word handed me some soap-filled scouring pads. They did the trick. And while I do not know how common the behavior of my friends the Vonkemans might be, I know I was impressed by the care and attention they give to a young man with a congenital heart disease whom they have befriended, whom they often call or write to, and whom every year they invite to spend a week with them on Schiermonnikoog. The state provides this man, Willem de Zoeten, with free medicine, doctors, and specialist advice, but the Vonkemans provide him with many opportunities to be happy.

I think if the world were coming to an end, I would go to Holland not because the apocalypse—as Heine suggested—would happen later there, but because the Dutch might well have worked out a way of forestalling it. If it was by flood, they'd certainly have their boats and houseboats ready, and the most terrible conflagration wouldn't get far with all that water. If I were sick and impecunious, Holland would be the place I would choose to recover in. If I were an old man of slender means and no longer much energy, Holland I know is the country in which I would be treated with respect while I sat on a canal bank and fished and dreamed and watched the boats go by. If I were dead, and a dead foreigner who had done something for Holland, like the men of the 1st British Airborne Division who died at Oosterbeek and Arnhem, Holland is the country where my bones would confidently lie in cared-for ground.

However Dutch care originates—in a strong sense of family responsibility, as witnessed by those birthday calendars hanging inside the toilet door; or in a knowledge, born on the dikes, that every man and his spade are the keeper and protector of every other man—the Dutch care well, and in an age of increasing numbers of people and more complex demands and services, they seem to care wisely and efficiently. In the first years of the Second World War the Ministry of Social Affairs put into effect a form of medical insurance called the Sick Fund. Under this system roughly 71 per cent of the population is insured with private, nonprofit associations, which pay the costs of all medical care for those insured with them. Everyone who earns less than 11,500 guilders a year must by law be insured; it costs an amount equal to about 6 per cent of a person's wages, and is paid half by the employee, half by the employer. The insurance associations pay hospitals, druggists, dentists, midwives, and doctors for the services they render. Family doctors receive a per-capita fee for everyone on their lists, and people can change their doctor every six months if they so desire; a doctor can also refuse to take a person on his list.

In community psychiatric care the Dutch have been pioneers. The mental health sections of their larger city health departments have developed psychiatric first aid services, with a number of teams—each composed of a social psychiatrist and a nurse—available to answer calls for help in acute cases, day or night. "This may be a severe emotional upset in a family home, an epileptic seizure, trouble with a mental defective, a suicidal attempt or depressive or excited behaviour," writes a Dutch health authority. "The service is very effective, and succeeds in keeping a good many patients out of hospital."

The institutions, however, are there if needed: 61,000

general hospital beds, 26,848 psychiatric hospital beds, 10,943 places in homes for the feebleminded, and 60,788 places in day schools for handicapped children. In any event, whether because the facilities are extensive or because the country is small, one is aware of places where people are looked after. At Katwijk on the seafront was a sanatorium for spastics. In museums and zoos one sees groups of handicapped children. They are taken to beaches and parks and on excursion boats on the Friesland lakes. In the woods near Arnhem there is a home for physically disabled people who can't live in an ordinary community—a home which is in fact a village, where each of the four hundred and fifty residents has his own room (there are eight separate buildings), and where there is a workshop, gym, library, central kitchen, supermarket, post office, barber shop, and gas station. Most of the residents of Het Dorp, as this community is called, are confined to wheelchairs, but they can go around Het Dorp on a street that is heated and glass-covered. All residents can come or go if they are able, and some work in Arnhem. Many pay their share of expenses; the rest is contributed by the government and the municipalities the residents come from. More than half the eleven million guilders cost of Het Dorp was raised in a national twenty-four-hour appeal, and now two similar villages are being planned.

I spent a morning in Amsterdam's municipal orphanage, which is on the edge of the city between the Bos and the Olympic Stadium. This children's home is a low, sprawling structure, built like a large Roman villa with a series of little rooms and bigger rooms honeycombed

around square courtyards. Most of the courtyards are
partly open on one side—the effect is of space that is
secure but can be easily left or entered. Each unit of the
building is roofed by a single large concrete cupola or a
series of small concrete cupolas, 336 in all, low dome or
dunelike shapes that give the roof a North African look.

My guide to the orphanage was Mr. Adema, its treas-
urer, a short, jovial man who told me that he had in fact
few orphans in his charge: perhaps four or five out of
one hundred and twenty-five children. Most of the children, from babies to the age of twenty, were wards of
societies that looked after broken families—sometimes
their mothers were in hospital or their fathers in jail. In
most cases they would stay at the "orphanage" for a year
or so until their home life improved. Even now thirty
lived out, with foster families, and all the school-age
children went off every day to normal Amsterdam
schools. The home was staffed by thirty people, including nurses, teachers, and social workers, and run by a
board of trustees, as it and its predecessor in the center
of the old city have been run since the seventeenth century. "We are well endowed," said Mr. Adema, "but then
most Dutch orphanages are. Rich men in our country
have always felt obliged to leave land and bonds to
places that look after children, the sick, or old people.
And Dutch towns take pride in building homes for
them. We get quite a few trustees coming here for advice because they have a fine orphanage and not enough
orphans—people don't die like they used to, or else relatives want to look after the children."

Other constant visitors to the home are architects, for

the building has become Holland's star architectural attraction. It was designed by Aldo van Eyck. Some Dutch colleagues describe Mr. van Eyck, tactfully, as a poet, but he is clearly a man who, in this building, has thought hard and originally about children. It is, to begin with, a building you can wander in, as I did with Mr. Adema, down a few steps where the change of level has been neatly emphasized by a line of bright blue ceramic tile at the edge of the top step, up a low ramp where bicycles can be wheeled, and along corridors that are like covered streets, the light and grass of a courtyard coming through high windows on one side, and the other walls built with the familiar brick of Dutch pavements —sandy purple-grey bricks with wide strips of mortar between them. Overhead there are portlights letting in broad shafts of sun. The corridors link big indoor courtyards, fine for riding bicycles in on rainy days. In fact, it is a building that can be played in. It is a permissive building. The only formality is the staircase leading to the meeting room of the trustees (from which there is a fine view of the Saharan rooftops), and where the slightly polished note is beautifully maintained by several fine pieces of seventeenth-century furniture and two handsome portraits of ladies who were regents of the orphanage in that time. Mr. Adema said the paintings were by Jacob Bakker, one of Rembrandt's students, and that the lack of eyebrows and eyelashes on the ladies was not a matter of faulty restoration but a common seventeenth-century condition, the result of singeing from blowing out candles.

In eight pavilions eight groups of children live as a kind of family. The sleeping rooms were designed by van Eyck (like many Dutch architects more fond of public expanse than private confines) as open dormitories, but the children preferred their own spaces, particularly when the family was of widespread age with small children and teenagers together. "Even if his own room is tiny," Mr. Adema said, "a child likes it better—he has something of his own." Mr. Adema added that some of these changes, which had resulted in partitions that didn't quite fit the original style and construction of the pavilions, were generally undertaken when Mr. van Eyck was away lecturing in America. There were a few other details that struck me as self-conscious, such as a wall of opaque glass brick which was suddenly parted by a pillar of transparent glass brick at a point where a drainpipe ran down from the roof behind the wall, and thus revealed the pipe in all its unfuzzy drainpipeness. Mr. Adema said that most visiting architects were thrilled by this stroke of architectural "honesty." Yet all the areas in which children played together seemed to me extraordinarily fine. There were big living rooms, with all sorts of plants and toys and objects, such as stoves children could actually cook on, with a little wall round three sides of the stove island so that small children couldn't burn their curious fingers. There were slight, thoughtful differences of floor level now and then, and shallow wells and pits. In the sides and backs of counters little mirrors were inset here and there, at different heights for different sizes of children. There were lots of cupboards to put and hide things in. A small bakery encouraged girls to make pancakes, and stools were set around for pancake eaters to sit on. One pavilion had a toy jail, with barred windows. Plants grew everywhere, and vines circled up the stands of tall lamps, which were the shape of tulips. I also saw hamsters and canaries, sandpits and swings, a puppet theater and a full-size canal punt, Beatle posters and an old copper pot from the original orphanage. There were rooms for homework and ironing and one which was, temporarily, a teenage discothèque. Each pavilion had a television set and several blackboards, and there were many works of art, among which I noticed a revolving tin sculpture by a fifteen-year-old girl, which stood in one inner courtyard, and, on a cork notice board, a drawing of houses by a seven-year-old boy. Mr. van Eyck's building is, despite its few errors and many brilliant innovations, a totally unpretentious home, and I thought it a nice complement that this child's house had low, dunelike roofs.

It was a schoolday, and only a few children were around; several toddlers bustling around on tricycles, and a baby crying. Dr. Fiedeldy Dop would have approved. "The children can come and go as if this were their own house," said Mr. Adema. "Of course, for some things like going to the movies, they have to get the permission of the lady in charge of their family; but very little is forbidden. The boys go off to football games and the girls to ballet lessons. If a child has the aptitude and wants to study a foreign language, there are no difficulties. The doctor comes daily. We have a consulting psychologist and a dietitian and people out all the time interviewing for good foster families. We are also lucky to have a very good chef, Mr. de Liefde. *Liefde* —do you know what that means? *Liefde* is love."

❧

In Holland the stranger soon notices that the art of the country is present in its life, and as, after a while, one sees Mondrians in the landscape or Vermeers in the faces of young women, so one sees Rembrandt everywhere: in the bend of a stream, with a barn beside a tree; in a child toddling in front of its mother in the Vondelpark; or in an old lady bending to pour tea. In the work of Rembrandt, moreover, one sees a mirror of the Dutch notion that old age is good. In Holland to have reached ripe years is to have gained an accumulation of experience and concern, and to be worth respect and given peace. There are no euphemisms in Dutch for being old —no "senior citizen," "golden ager," or even the rather belittling British term "pensioner." Often, in the course of arranging to see someone, I would be told, "No, don't come that day—I'm taking my aunt to the Concertgebouw," or, "Make it the following week, will you? My father and I are going birdwatching on Texel." Although the Dutch are in the vanguard of the old-age explosion, with more and more old people living longer, using more hospital space, and requiring more government expenditure, the Dutch show no signs of rejecting their old people or cutting them off, the way people of other countries sometimes seem to, for fear of being old themselves. One can perhaps add to the reasons for Dutch longevity (which might include bicycle riding, margarine eating, and good, inexpensive health service) the fact that the Dutch enjoy old age. Old people are not deserted and unwanted; on the other hand, they retain a certain carefree independence.

Sir William Temple once enjoyed a visit to a home for aged seamen at Enkhuisen, and similar pleasures can be had today. Indeed, one quick way to escape from the elbow-to-elbow turmoil of Randstad towns and cities is to take sanctuary in the courtyard of a *hofje,* a group of little almshouses where old people live. These cottages are generally one story high and surround a garden with a well in it. The *hofje* at Katwijk formed a square which you entered through an archway, and though the little houses in this case were rather unattractive, the garden within provided a splendid refuge from the hurly-burly of the seafront promenade. In Amsterdam, just off the famous shopping area of the Kalverstraat, is the *Begijnhof.* Here the three-, four-, or even five-story houses stand like the high sides of a ship around a ship-shaped garden. As in a Dutch ship, in every way a reaction to the flat and linear landscape, there are no straight lines. The houses tilt and lean, no two alike, one wooden, some red brick, some with painted façades, each with its own small front garden and wooden fence. The side wall of the Presbyterian church slants in tangentially as if to bolster or reassure the houses. A Catholic church is camouflaged inside one of the houses, as it had to be once during the Reformation, though now a small notice board advertises its presence. In flowerbeds that are not too elegant grow lilac, pansies, bluebells; there are several apple trees and a great chestnut. No traffic sounds. Pigeons coo and a few old ladies scrub their stoops, wash their windows, or stand chatting, oblivious to the occasional tourist who wanders in and drifts around in a pleasurable daze.

Some *hofjes* began in the Middle Ages. The *Begijnhof*s were cloisters where lay women could devote themselves to the religious life, and there were also *gasthuisen*, set up by private donations and bequests, for sheltering the poor and the aged. Although most of the religious houses were dissolved in the Reformation, the spirit carried over into the establishment of many new *hofjes* in the seventeenth and eighteenth centuries. Leiden had twenty, Amsterdam seventy-five. Founding a *hofje* was a way of doing good and also of setting up a monument to oneself, with one's name inscribed over the entrance arch. It was a form of charity which also afforded commissions to Dutch painters, who were asked to portray the founder and the trustees or regents who administered his will. Roughly one hundred and twenty-five old groups of *hofjes* are still being run for the benefit of some four thousand elderly people in them.

I went one day with Mr. Hoog, the retired tulip grower, to look at the *hofje* in Haarlem of which he is the regent. It was sequestered in a side street behind a high brick wall. The narrow archway was topped by a carved stone with incised gold lettering on an azure blue surround: *Frans Loenen Hoefjen aᵒ 1625*. Inside, past the pump which every *hofje* courtyard has, there were gnarled old white-blossomed pear trees; here the flowers were daffodils and early tulips. The pavement in front of the L-shaped row of little houses was made of thin yellow bricks, laid on their sides in sand. Each little house had one large front window, with flowers in pots on the sill, and a true Dutch door, the top half of which was often open to let in the air and sun. The sounds in the courtyard were of birds and elderly ladies twittering, and as we passed, one woman leaned over her door to thank Mr. Hoog for a garden seat he had given them, and which was already standing under one of the pear trees. The third wall of the courtyard was the side of the neighboring Lutheran church, against which espalier pears had been trained.

"There are forty old women here," said Mr. Hoog, as we entered the doorway of the final cottage in the row; it was in use as the regent's room. There was a cupboard full of fine crystal port glasses, and a portrait of Frans Loenen, the founder, who looked as if he would miss the toasts and speech-making. "There was a little trouble with Frans Loenen's will, which was eventually sorted out, but today the interest on the capital he left has proved insufficient for all our needs, and we've had to look for more. We've been lucky to round up some extra legacies to help. Most of the old ladies have pensions, for that matter, and they pay a small admission fee, something less than two hundred dollars. Those who can, help meet the costs of light and heat. We have a long waiting list for admission—the ladies have to be widows or spinsters, and over 65, and we've found recently, since we got our new matron who belongs to the Salvation Army, that it helps to get in if you are a member of the Salvation Army too. But she is a good matron. She runs a tight ship, and the old women seem to like it here. They each have their own small house. It is a simple and a quiet place."

It is a tradition with life in it. Queen Wilhelmina turned a country house into a home for old people, and each town has its *hofje*. The group called New Ways of Living has a retirement home as one of its projects. In the new developments the accommodation for elderly people may not be so cherished and well worn, but it seems well integrated, built in low blocks of apartments, as at Pendrecht, or in terraces of small modern houses, set among blocks of flats and larger family houses, where children play and people go back and forth and there is more to do and see than the activities of one's contemporaries. Even so, the need for such accommodation is greater than the supply. Not in small towns, which can more easily cope with their own, but in larger cities with long waiting lists of old people. Twelve per cent of the population of Amsterdam is over sixty-five, and this figure will probably be 15 per cent by the end of the century. Many of these people can look after themselves, and some will be housed in such places as the new Bijlmermeer development, where they will have a flat of their own and a matron to assist them if they need. But others want a home that provides constant care, and Amsterdam is currently building facilities for four thousand old people in that condition. It has also established a central bureau to cope with the problems of the elderly, to collate the waiting lists of private, religious, and municipal homes, and to investigate the needs of old people so that those in most distress are helped first. In the past (I was told by Mr. Plemper of that bureau) many old people have gained admission to a home at the age of sixty-five and have lived in great good health and no real need for the next twenty years or so, while some who have been old and incapable have not found room. The average age of people presently in Amsterdam *hofjes* and homes is eighty-two—and if more modern homes are built like the Hospice Wallon, that high age might become higher still. The Hospice Wallon is run for members of the Huguenot church, and it is something of an exception in demanding that old people be in fairly good physical shape on admission; trained nursing staff is hard to get. But once people are in, there are facilities for keeping them as fit as can be: a gym, physical education classes, and such comforts as a ladies's hairdresser, library, laundry, and chapel. At the Hospice there were many thoughtful details of design: ramps instead of steps, places in bathrooms for nurses to wedge their feet while assisting invalids to get in or out of a bath; and timer switches which automatically turn off stoves in the kitchenettes of each room. The matron here was an energetic, personable lady who had been for eighteen years a nurse on a liner. She told me that in this building, which was five stories high and situated in south Amsterdam with a view of gardens and single-family houses, there were no problems with high-rise living; in fact, the residents coveted the top apartments. She said, "They want to be up high, preferably on the east side where they can see the sun come up in the morning."

❦

In some countries the best architecture is to be seen in private houses; in other countries it is in office buildings or banks. In Holland the best is in *hofjes*, hospices, and hostels, in new buildings like Aldo van Eyck's children's home or Herman Hertzberger's student hostel on the Weesperstraat in Amsterdam—a three-story rough concrete structure incorporating an arcade, a bookstore, a café, student rooms, and a strong feeling of being an enclosed street where young men and women can stand and talk, or sit and read; a place to meet, a place to make speeches, a place to think. Hertzberger has provided many benches and sills to sit on, and plenty of unfinished-looking surfaces on which he anticipated many posters would be stuck up—though perhaps not so many as have appeared, plastered one on top of another, giving the arcade and open stairwell a large collage-by-Kurt Schwitters effect. At any rate, despite a difference in age of two hundred and fifty years, Hertzberger's contemporary concrete building is informed by the same humanity that seems to exist in the *hofjes*, the same idea of giving form to a community in which man is encouraged to be independent. I spent an afternoon in Friesland at Poptaslot, near Leeuwarden, a semifortified country house which had belonged in the early eighteenth century to Dr. Popta, a rich lawyer and landowner. I visited the room where Dr. Popta used to receive his rents from his tenant farmers, and I saw the desk with a hidden drawer where he kept his money. The desk top was of inlaid marble, for Dr. Popta to tap the silver on and make sure it hadn't been devalued with tin. And later I walked across the moat to the other end of the formal garden and looked at what Dr. Popta's money had endowed: two large courtyards of absolutely spic-and-span deluxe *hofjes*, the terraced cottages built of pale pink brick, with pink roses, white fences, elegant lampposts, double doors, green shutters, and caps, like the caps of old women, over the chimney pots.

❦ 20 ❦

As the country grows more urban and more complicated, a feature that becomes more and more important is the mechanism of compromise—the machinery by which people with different demands and occupations and interests manage to talk to one another and arrive at agreements. Where there is no talk and no agreement the modern city tends to stop. It is therefore interesting that except for one rare month in 1960 when three building unions went out, the last major widespread strike that took place in Holland was in Amsterdam in 1941, and was chiefly directed at the Nazi registration of the Jews. Although there are occasional wildcat strikes, they are less frequent than in other industrial countries. Experts say that the Dutch workman has a traditional fear of his boss and is temperamentally disinclined to strike; but this may be in part because he knows he gets more results out of a conflict which has been localized at a meeting table, where his representatives and those of the management can have it out with each other. Even at the meeting table there doesn't seem to be a great deal of drama. Dr. W. F. de Gaay Fortman, professor of Labor Law at the Free University in Amsterdam and an authority on Dutch industrial relations, recalls in a 1960 issue of the quarterly *Delta* what he calls "one tense night meeting" to decide how far consumer consumption and industrial investment expenditure should be limited to prevent a currency crisis. This was in 1953. The trade unions were prepared to accept a lowering of real income for their men, but didn't want to go as far as the employers. Negotiations staggered on through the night, sometimes to the point of breakdown, but never actually breaking down. At dawn, both parties agreed with government representatives that real wages would be dropped 5 per cent, not by actually cutting the wages, but by removing the subsidies on necessities like bread and milk.

That perspicacious gentleman, Sir William Temple, observed that although the Dutch were naturally "cold and heavy," and by no means vivacious conversationalists, yet they had their talents. With them, "Thought moves slower and heavier, but thereby the impressions of it are deeper, and last longer." Democracy and drama are antithetical. It might in fact be said that a country whose politics are consistently interesting is a country unready for democratic procedure. It is quite possible to live for six months in Holland and not know the name of the Prime Minister (though a little harder to avoid knowing the name of the Foreign Minister); no one assassinates politicians in Holland. A truly democratic disposition, as Professor Huibert Drion of the University of Leiden points out (in *Delta*, Summer 1968), "presupposes an acceptance of compromise." For that reason it often seems unattractive to intellectuals and to students for a so-called democratic society. Democracy lacks a crisp, architecturally ordered system. Its carefulness is unromantic and frustrating. Democracy, writes Professor Drion, choosing his metaphors most Dutchly, "moves forward with the heavy caution of a man who knows he is answerable for his actions."

The Dutch came late to the Industrial Revolution, but perhaps no later than other countries to a realization of the gulf between workers and bourgeoisie. In the late nineteenth century agitation was often violent. Socialist unions opposed the whole structure of Dutch society; in 1918 there were street battles in Amsterdam and an attempted *putsch*. Queen Wilhelmina came into the streets to try and calm the demonstrators. But since then Catholic and Protestant unions have taken their share of the workers's support. There is no closed shop in Holland, and the fact that various unions compete for the allegiance of working men perhaps has helped collective negotiation take the place of direct action. The Dutch sociologist J. Goudsblom quotes approvingly his German colleague, Theodor Geiger, who mentions "the institutionalization of class antagonism." Goudsblom writes: "The conflicts between labor and management have not disappeared, but both parties have conceded in the acceptance of a set of rules providing for settlement by orderly means. In the Netherlands this development has gone further than in most countries."

The institutions are, first, the Foundation of Labor, which is made up of the central employers' organizations and trade-union federations, and, second, the Social and Economic Council, which has fifteen members from private industry, fifteen from unions, and fifteen independent experts appointed by the government. The Council provides the constantly operating negotiating machinery. The government is required by law to seek its advice on all important social and economic questions; and the Council, on its own initiative, can give advice to the government whenever it feels like it. Until 1954 the government, with this advice, laid down wage rates for all industry, but since then the policy has been relaxed to a point where the government only interferes when it feels a wage proposal is contrary to the national interest. In Holland throughout this postwar period wages and prices have been fairly successfully kept down. Industrial investment has been promoted, together with the sale of Dutch goods on the world market. There has been a conscious effort to pursue long-term benefits for everyone, rather than short-term benefits for small groups of either employers or employees. Two results of this have been full employment and a very small loss of working days from strikes. (In 1963, the Netherlands with a population of a little more than twelve million lost 38,000 working days. In the same year the United States, with a population sixteen times greater, lost 16,100,000 working days—roughly twenty times more. The Netherlands' figures in this respect are also a little lower than those of Sweden, half that of Denmark, and a great deal lower than those of other European countries.)

Dr. Fortman writes: "Industrial relations in the Netherlands are based on a deeply rooted consciousness that employers and workers are not each other's natural enemies, but that they are interdependent and hence must cooperate. Mutual consultation is thus the characteristic of Dutch industrial relations." One suspects, however, that now and then the Dutch worker feels out of touch with his union leaders, who seem to be always consulting one another and not—he feels—talking to him. Hence what strikes there are are wildcat strikes. Many workmen don't belong to a union at all, for that matter, or don't participate very actively in the union they belong to. The responsible, care-full society has brought about such extensive medical and social improvements that some unions feel their entire *raison d'être* has been undermined, although in fact a lot remains to be done in improving the communications and conditions in individual factories. Some of the "bosses" realize this. Mr. J. Bosma, president of the Federation of Netherlands' Industry, noted recently the arrival in industry of younger, better-educated men. "The older generation was used to accepting orders. The younger generation on the other hand is less prepared to accept orders without knowing something of their implication. . . . The manager must be willing to discuss problems with those groups in his factory which are able to give a positive contribution, before he takes a decision. And he must be willing to delegate responsibility, even to the lowest ranks." Menno Brandsma, the polder biologist, told me of the conferences he had with young workers on his staff, with the idea of getting them to understand why he needed, say, an accurate count of the number of seeds on an ear of reed, and that while speed was not important, precision was. "When they understood this," said Mr. Brandsma, "and my reasons for asking it, they felt responsible for doing it the way I wanted. They enjoyed doing it."

❧

With education, prosperity, and a strong bourgeois tradition, the proletariat is withering away in Holland; the political atmosphere is highly unrevolutionary. Risk to a very large degree has been removed from life.

Priestly celibacy and the proposed Amsterdam Metro sometimes seem to be the only real sources of controversy. Security and safety appear to have been achieved at the expense of zip and zing. There is no bounce in a featherbed.

Take, for example, a traffic junction in any Randstad town. Two roads cross: hence cars come from four directions, bicycles and *brommers* arrive in their own four tracks, and pedestrians cross in eight possible ways. If you want to make a left turn in a car, you have to think about it well in advance of the intersection, moving into the left of two lanes: then, at the junction, you have to wait for a green arrow to light up, pointing left. (This may be a long wait, because the lights are arranged to let people move safely rather than speedily.) And if by chance you find yourself mistakenly in the left-hand lane, with the green arrow beckoning you to the left, you had better obey its signal. One day in the outskirts of The Hague, in heavy traffic, I missed the road markings indicating that I was in a lane which, at the next junction, would have to make a left turn. I didn't want to make a left turn. I didn't know where it would lead me. So when the left-turn green arrow came on, I drove straight ahead as soon as I saw that it was safe to do so and no cars from the other direction were making their left turns in front of me. At once whistles blew, policemen ran out of hiding and jumped up and down, and other car drivers honked their horns in jealous anger. There was no hot pursuit, but you would have thought from all the commotion that I had taken a spade and begun to attack the dikes, the very foundations of Dutch society.

"We had the loveliest identity cards during the war," writes Professor Nordholt, alluding somewhat sardonically to the pleasure the Dutch take in the creation of red tape. His colleague, Professor van Rooijen, says: "Every Dutch inhabitant is well aware that he is caught up in a network of rules and regulations aimed at ensuring his responsible behavior within an increasingly compact concentration of people. The intense population pressure demands that he march neatly in step, for in order to function smoothly the community cannot allow any crowding or blocking." Some 14 per cent of the Dutch working population is now employed by the government, and the percentage of the national income devoted to government expenditure has risen from 10 per cent in 1900 to 25 per cent in 1960, and is still climbing. The Dutch complain that they are always filling up forms. They make such remarks as, "Oh, we have to pay taxes just for looking over our shoulders." (In fact, they pay less income tax than the Swedes and have lower social security payments than the French.) "Everything here is regulated except breathing," said Ivo Blom, longing for his Corsican mountainside, where he would undoubtedly sit and dream of Holland—Holland where a doctor will always see you, a hospital admit you, trains will always run, and the garbage will always be collected and one's friends will be waiting in a smoky pub to talk of red tape and regulations and who is going to be on next year's list of government grants.

Although I have no figures for the amount of litigation, the Dutch consider themselves a litigious race, always going to court to get rulings on all manner of agreements, regulations, and contracts. An agency through which we rented the houses of several teachers in Holland had a ponderous list of people who would sit on an arbitration board to hear any complaints of tenant against landlord, or landlord against tenant. The Dutch need for insurance, security, and associations to which they *belong*, may have some connection with their precarious situation—a below-sea-level insecurity. And of course there are pleasures to be taken in things being well regulated, things being *just so*, like neatly coiled lines on a yacht. But in that case one's infuriation is all the greater when everything is just so save for one crucial element, as in our generally well-designed little shower room at Katwijk where the sink, in itself well designed, was three times too large for that particular space and was therefore triply annoying. The need to belong can also be irritating. In order to get the best magazine with details of boats to hire and where to go to sail them it is necessary to be a member of a national camping organization. Holland is a democracy, but its citizens are compelled to vote, with the penalty of a fine if they don't.

I went one night to an organ concert in St. Bavo's, the great church of Haarlem. Printed in the program was a prominent note: *Gedurende het gehele orgelconcert is het verboden door de kerk to lopen.* There were translations into German, French, and English, the latter being:

"It is forbidden to walk in the church all during the concert." Halfway through, in a pause between a Bach Prelude and a Partita by Gunter Raphael, a little girl sitting in front of me wanted to go to the bathroom. Her mother reacted slowly. They had got only a few steps away from their seats when the organ boomed again. Immediately the mother stopped and pulled the child to a halt. They stood like statues while the music played, and every time there was a moment of silence they took a few quick steps. Every time it began again they froze. After a while, when they were still little more than halfway from their seats to the church door, I was bursting with the desire to scream at the woman, "For God's sake, take your child and walk out of this church like a human being." Instead for ten minutes she behaved like a puppet, and the child, being a good little Dutch woman, hid her anguish.

❧

The Dutch attribute to themselves, as their preeminent characteristic, independence—so a Dutch television poll decided not long ago. Are they in fact independent and full of *onrust*? Aren't they the most placid people? "The Dutch are the most controlled people in the world," a young Dutch student named Carl van Lennop said recently. "The Dutch are told what to do in every sphere of life." Van Lennop was in an Amsterdam jail when he made these pronouncements and the *misè-en-*

scène may have been influencing him. But he was also a Provo, one of a small group of Dutch people who from 1965 to May 1967 brought a sense of risk, unrest, and revolution to the forefront of Dutch life. Provo seemed to some to be the anti-Dutchman made flesh, and to others to be a flowering of much that is right in Holland. One pundit, a forty-seven-year-old professor at The Hague, wondered whether Provo might not be "a phenomenon that foreshadows tomorrow's culture of the Western world."

Some Provos were not young. One of the Provo candidates for the 1966 Amsterdam City Council election was a then sixty-eight-year-old writer, Jef Last. However, most of the twenty-five or so people who were the core of the loosely bound movement called Provo were in their twenties or early thirties—people like Luud Schimmelpenninck, an industrial designer; Irene van Wetering, housewife, mother of two, married to Jan Donner; and Robert Jasper Grootveld, a former window cleaner. They were people of different views, backgrounds, and temperaments, sharing perhaps two things not usually considered "typically Dutch"—a sense of humor, and a desire to *provoke* by their actions a social or political response. Some always dressed in white. Some met in a cellar, or in the barge Hashimin, moored to the Jacob Cats kade.

Grootveld partly inspired Provo's beginnings in the summer of 1964, when he held happenings ("mumbling crazy incantations," according to one observer) at the statue *Het Lieverdje* ("The Little Rascal"), which stands on the Spui in the center of old Amsterdam. It is the figure of a street urchin, wearing a peaked cap and tumble-down knee socks, and was given to the city by a cigarette manufacturer. Grootveld, painted as a clown, declared that the statue was a symbol of "the addicted consumer of tomorrow." His followers proceeded to paint large letter K's, for *Kanker* (the Dutch word for cancer), on cigarette billboard advertisements all over the city. Another monument which recieved attention, in the form of white paint being splashed all over it, was that erected to General van Heutsz, who led Dutch forces in the war (1873–1905) that put down the independent Sumatran state of Achin. Elsewhere the semihooligan fringe that collects around such natural leaders lit bonfires in the porticoes of the royal palace on the Dam and generally made a public nuisance of themselves whenever they could. But during 1965 the serious Provos who were coming together (though their political intentions were severally anarchist, republican, and utopian) found an issue ripe for provocations—the engagement of Dutch Princess Beatrix to German Claus von Amsberg. And from this point, the Amsterdam municipal authorities reacted to Provo with thick-skinned burgherish ineptitude, while the Provos became more and more famous. Their magazine *Provo* was confiscated, and achieved much wider circulation than before. The weekly Saturday night happening around *Het Lieverdje* was interrupted by the police, which brought forth more and more spectators, generally sympathetic to the Provos. A few smoke bombs were thrown at the wedding procession of Beatrix and Claus, which the government, with vast insensitivity to the anti-German feeling of Amsterdam, allowed to take place there and to be solemnized by the burgomaster himself, Mr. Gijsbert van Hall. (The awareness of the municipal authorities may be judged from the fact that they considered using the Anne Frank house as a temporary police station on the festive day.) In April, in the course of a season of protests and police arrests, a girl named Koosje Koster was arrested for handing out free raisins to people on a city street.

In the Amsterdam municipal elections which took took place in June 1966, the Provos, winning 13,000 votes or 2½ per cent of the total, were granted (under the proportional representation system) one seat on the forty-five member City Council. A cause of their popularity were the Provo white plans, which put forward ways of improving life in Amsterdam. The white bicycle plan proposed closing the center of the old city to motor traffic and providing every year twenty thousand white bicycles which could be used by everyone; and the Provos made a start on this by painting some of their own bicycles white and putting them at the public disposal. The bicycles were confiscated by the police. The white chimney plan was the Provo answer to air pollution. It suggested appropriate fees, payable to the community, for the discharge of alien substances into the air, and put forward such technical, perhaps tongue-in-cheek, details as "the color of the fumes must be lighter than no. 1 of the Ringelman scale." The white wives plan was concerned with illegitimacy, abortions, and shotgun marriages. It proposed clinics at district health centers where girls and women could obtain contraceptives and advice; it also proposed that school medical officers let adolescent girls know of the existence of the clinic. "Couples with two children should be warned that they will be acting irresponsibly if they have another child," wrote Irene Donner van Wetering, mother of two. "I cannot see why underdeveloped countries should be the only ones to profit widely from the newest scientific methods of birth control. If these measures are carried out, girls will have the opportunity of acquiring experience in making love from adolesence onwards. . . . it is hardly necessary to point out that it is completely irresponsible, if not shocking, to enter marriage as a virgin—you can't 'tell chalk from cheese,' you are expected to take and keep the first man you meet, and there are absolutely no guarantees that you and he will be sexually suited."

There were other white plans: the white chicken plan (*kip*, or chicken, being Provo slang for police or fuzz), which suggested the disarming of Dutch police and making them social workers to distribute bandages, medicines, contraceptives, "Royal Dutch oranges and chicken drumsticks for the starving provotariat"; the white housing plan, proposing the use of condemned dwellings as free temporary accommodations for young people, the return of old houses in the central city to their previous use as residences from their present use as offices, and the preservation of the open-air flea market on the Waterlooplein—the site designated for the new town hall; and not least, the white corpse plan, an antitraffic terror

measure by which the police accident squad was to be
equipped with chalk, chisel, hammer, and a bucket of
white mortar. Whenever a car flattened a pedestrian, the
police were to trace the victim's outline with chalk on
the "merciless asphalt." The car driver was to hack out
with hammer and chisel the victim's silhouette and fill it
in with the white mortar. "Then, perhaps, all the pro-
spective murderers approaching the scene of the disaster
will let up on the gas for just a moment."

From the summer of 1966 to May 1967 there were
further arrests, marches in support of striking construction workers, demonstrations at the United States con-
sulate against America's Vietnam policy, more issues of
the paper *Provo*, the establishment of several government commissions to investigate the situation, the firing
of the Amsterdam police chief, the dismissal of Burgomaster van Hall, and finally, on May 13, 1967, a gather-
ing in the Vondelpark, where some Provos decided to dis-
band the movement and others decided to continue. The
result was perhaps only a muddle-headed dilution of the
state of flux Provo had always been in, but since then the
Provo paper has not been issued. One Provo said: "We
have buried Provo. He is dead."

Yet there are no homes for retired Provos in Holland,
as of this moment, and in many ways Provo lives on.
Some of the most unlikely people—who seem superficially hyperbourgeois—are to be heard expressing sym-
pathy for Provo, what it was, and the people involved in
it. Enneus Heerma, who is a member of the Farmer's
Party, a conservative political group to which his father

has always belonged, told me: "Provo had a lot of good ideas, though perhaps they were expressed in a rather extreme way. For one thing, it helped make new connections between Amsterdam citizens and the city councilors. The old stuffy, remote burgher tradition had gone on too long." The Dutch seem almost proud of Provo—it showed they had their own radical, whimsical spirit.

The attention given the Provos did not please everyone. Dutch political scientists got worked up about the Provo claims to be anarchist or in the line of earlier Dutch movements such as the Eel rebellion of 1886 or the potato riots of 1917. "Workers threatened by hunger and need," wrote sociologist Ger Harmsen, "are not to be compared with bored and artificially agitated youths who do not know the meaning of want and deprivation." Yet the Provos did want something and did feel deprived. "What really makes us mad is the individual's lack of influence on events. A happening is an attempt to seize at least the little part in things that you ought to have and that the authorities try to take away from you." The Provo who said this, Roel van Duyn, also told an interviewer: "We know our actions are useless; we are quite ready to believe that neither Johnson nor Kosygin will listen to us, and for that very reason we are free to do what we like." In some ways the Provos seemed to be protesting against their freedom, the lack of social disorder, and the very comfort of the Dutch version of a welfare state. And despite their feelings of deracination and absurdity, they did get listened to, they did influence some events, and they did force a number of issues into the open where they had to be discussed. Given the publicity of confiscation, their paper *Provo* sold thousands of copies. Their provocations of authority caused a great deal of official soul-searching and eventually a reshuffling of the hidebound Amsterdam police force. Some youths who might otherwise have been full-time delinquents engaged in petty crime, were to be found cranking out copies of *Provo* or taking part in relatively peaceful Vietnam protests. Winning a seat on the City Council showed that the individual could have some influence on political events. In fact, their supporters claim that Provos or the active political climate got city councilors to work harder—councilors are paid for attendance by the hour, and the annual Council accounts indicate that they are getting more pay than they used to. Moreover, Provo involved people with much to give: designers like Schimmelpenninck, architects like Aldo van Eyck, and writers like Harry Mulisch. In some ways, dealing with the new community-dominated society, it was a conservationist movement. It protested against the depopulation of old Amsterdam and the replacement of houses with large offices and banks. (At one demonstration to denounce the construction of a bank in a historic square, Robert Grootveld, the happener, found himself on the same platform, making the same points, as A. J. d'Ailly, a former burgomaster of the city.) Another serious result of Provo was that Dutch laws governing freedom of expression were looked into, and found wanting in regard to freedom of demonstration.

Provo, one can now suspect, was itself provoked by the possibility suddenly inherent in Dutch society: this

was the first generation unterrified by authority or by
fear of poverty, uncommitted to consumer passions for
cars (which the provos take for granted) or security (of
which they feel they have enough). It was a rebellion of
haves rather than have-nots. Many even wanted to *give*
things away, which struck terror in some Dutch souls.
Sociologists were thus given a chance to talk of generation gaps, the welfare state, and situations where "the
combination of rapid technological change and continuous political apathy leads easily to that kind of protest,"
and to wonder what post-welfare-state world Provo fore-
shadowed. And some of Provo's adherents wondered too.
Constant Nieuwenhuys, the fifty-year-old artist, architect,
and writer, has been preoccupied with what he calls New
Babylon, a world of plenty "in which man no longer
toils, but plays." Constant (as he signs his work) thinks
dawn has not quite broken on this new world: man is still
bound to the idea of work as his great fulfillment, even
though the work may be performed by machine, and he
is still as yet only a semiplayer, sketching the future.
"But his outlines of the new world to come are important
in that at last he deliberately turns away from the utili-
tarian world in which creativeness was only an escape
and a protest, and that he becomes the interpreter of
the new man, *homo ludens.*"

Constant's theories otherwise incorporate a sincere and
not particularly original attack on traffic in towns, and
what strikes me as a misunderstood view of what
Ebenezer Howard's garden cities were all about—a mis-
understanding based, I think, on the dormitory developments of Amsterdam rather than Howard's writings. In

any event, it is Constant's belief that a person's living quarters become less important to him "as his radius of action expands and his amount of leisure time increases." The new man is going to be increasingly nomadic. Present youthful protest is chiefly directed "at the recovery of social space—the street—so that the contacts essential for play may be established."

Despite such marvels as Europoort, the Dutch are by no means in the forefront of automation. Most Dutchmen work forty-two hours a week, and five and a half days is not uncommon. Yet the approaching age of leisure has received full attention. Concern with it is bringing about the rapid opening up of new woods and recreation areas. As long ago as 1938 the Dutch historian Johan Huizinga published a book called *Homo Ludens*, a study of the play-element in culture. To Huizinga (who also wrote *Erasmus of Rotterdam* and *The Waning of the Middle Ages*), man was not about to become *homo ludens*; he always had been. "The spirit of playful competition is, as a social impulse, older than culture itself and pervades all life like a veritable ferment. Ritual grew up in sacred play; poetry was born in play and nourished on play; music and dancing were pure play. Wisdom and philosophy found expression in words and forms derived from religious contests. The rules of warfare, the conventions of noble living were built up on play patterns. . . . Civilisation . . . does not come *from* play like a babe detaching itself from the womb: it arises *in* and *as* play, and never leaves it."

Huizinga's book is in itself perhaps a scholarly piece

of play. For it is interesting that as the author approached the present, where contemporary reality rather than documents and ideas begins to rule, he finds his theory a little harder to justify. "The nineteenth century seems to leave little room for play." Sport becomes more and more commercial. And war—well, high above the World War I trenches, there were airmen challenging each other, and that was a game. But the conclusion slowly forced itself upon him that the play-element in culture has been on the wane since the eighteenth century.

But what about life rather than culture? Surely, in the past, man has been involved in a life of toil rather than one of play—the play Huizinga examines is in fact the distractions, escapes, and conventions created to make that life more bearable. A civilization has had to come into being where the majority of people could in all earnestness, at leisure, consider themselves and their destiny, before the impulse to play could become as creative as the impulse to work. In Holland such a condition seems more likely today than it did in 1938. Listen to Bernhard de Vries, first Provo member of the Amsterdam City Council: "Provo is unique because it is the vanguard in a unique situation—that of a general state of welfare in which for the first time in history man has space to live his own life creatively. . . . To the homo ludens! Against abuse of power! Playfully onward toward a livable Amsterdam!"

❧ 21 ❧

AMSTERDAM: the city as an expression of care; the city, one could perhaps say, as a work of art. It is for the Dutch their most *gezellig* place. You have to be an Amsterdammer, and a Provo, to say *toward* a livable Amsterdam, for the 93 per cent of the population that does not live in the city, although they may be aware that the city has contemporary problems, believes that Amsterdam *is* livable: most of them would jump at the chance to live there. "Man, thinly scattered, makes a shift, but a bad shift, without many things," Dr. Johnson told Boswell. "It is being concentrated which produces high convenience." And what convenience to be concentrated in the city which is probably the best example of town planning in the world; the city which is a densely woven tissue of human relations, history, trade, and art, and an intricate fabric of brick, water, sand, and stone.

As European cities go, Amsterdam is not particularly ancient. The presence of a small sandbank, situated where the river Amstel joined the stretch of water called the IJ, encouraged the first medieval settlement of fishermen. In 1300, with trade being conducted on the spot, a local lord granted a town charter with rights to build ramparts and walls. The fifteenth century was notable for two great fires, one in 1421 which burned down a third of the town, and one in 1452 which burned three quarters of it. The sixteenth century brought real prosperity: the closing of the Scheldt by Hollanders, when the Spanish troops captured Antwerp in 1585, encouraged the transfer of trade from the southern Low Countries to the northern. Sugar refiners, diamond cutters, and merchants of all types left Antwerp for Amsterdam. The Spanish occupation of Portugal also forced the Dutch to find their own sea routes to the Indies for the silks and spices the Portuguese had formerly supplied. Moreover, the population explosion of the seventeenth century created great pockets of want, which the Dutch provided for and profited from. Ships packed the harbor, as Holland became not only the great trader with the East but the chief carrier for all of northern Europe, and the fount of exploration. Henry Hudson sailed in the *Half Moon* in 1609 from the Schreierstoren, in Amsterdam. An Exchange was built in 1608. The expansion of the city in those years was never matched: 15,000 people in 1580; 50,000 in 1600; 100,000 in 1620; and 200,000 in 1660. In 1650 the trade of the Netherlands exceeded that of all other European countries taken together, and Amsterdam had much of it. It was the Golden Age, the age of Rembrandt (1606–69), but also the age of gold, much of which was plowed back in. Sir William Temple, the British ambassador, noted that in no other town anywhere were "Strength, Beauty and Convenience better provided for, nor with unlimited Expence, than in this, by the Magnificence of their Publick Buildings, as Stad-

house and Arsenals," also hospitals, canals, bastions and
ramparts, "and the neatness, as well as convenience, of
their Streets, so far as can be compassed in so great a
confluence of industrious People."

The form of the city was set in those years. In 1611 a
plan was drawn up to give the city expansion room in
the century to come, with four semicircular canals, each
one a step further from the center: Heerengracht,
Keizersgracht, Prinsengracht, Singel. (The room was
urgently needed, housing and traffic being the major
urban problems of that as of this century. Amsterdam
experimented with one-way streets in 1615, and for a
while forbade private carriages to circulate within the
city limits, so packed were the streets and narrow
bridges with wagons and freight sledges.) Earth taken
from the new canals by spade and wheelbarrow was used
to build up the ground between one canal and another
so that buildings could be erected; piles, however, had
to be driven into this raised ground to bear the foundations of residences and warehouses. Water from the
soggy ground drained into the canals. Water reflected
the brickwork of bridges and the leaning façades of
canalside buildings. Water was the medium of transport
which brought wealth to the mechants, giving them the
wherewithal to encourage the expansion of the city and
build their simple yet elegant houses with step gables,
neck gables, spout gables, and bell gables. Form followed
function and necessity, but it was embellished by enthusiasm and pride. Trees planted along the canal banks
held the banks together, shaded the paved streets, and

cast their own ever-changing reflections on the still water.

If truth is beauty, in architecture it is a twofold truth. It is an expression of what is practical, what works; and it is an expression of the way things work, the energy of a particular people. In Amsterdam's case, the need to move cargoes and to build permanent shelters on unstable ground. I have spent many days walking along those streets, listening to the trams rattle and the *rondvaart* launches blow their horns. There are a hundred canals in Amsterdam and six hundred and thirty-five bridges. There are a hundred thousand trees and just over a thousand houseboats. The trams whip along the narrow streets, with a legal right-of-way over other traffic that doesn't prevent cars and bicycles from fighting a good fight at every constricted streetcorner or junction. There are two universities, forty-one museums, four hundred pubs, sixty-nine Chinese restaurants, fifteen street organs, and five thousand buildings of the seventeenth and eighteenth centuries. Daily, Amsterdam has twenty-two deaths and forty-four births, three divorces and twenty marriages. Things in good proportion.

And yet walking around this city one finds anxieties like those of Bernhard de Vries. The flea market on the Waterlooplein is going to make room for a new town hall (while the first town hall on the Dam is still a little-used royal palace). People are particularly upset by the Netherlands Bank in the Fredericksplein, a not unhandsome piece of glass and steel curtain-wall architecture situated on part of what was once a pleasant, formal park. The bank, they feel, is seriously out of scale with the surrounding old city, a structure in the damn-your-eyes tradition of the Amsterdam Stock Exchange, whose massive blind brick west wall casts a great gloom on the Damrak, the main street leading from the Dam to the Central Station. Designed by the early twentieth-century Dutch architect Berlage, the Exchange has a notable reputation among architectural historians and connoisseurs of esoteric "transitional" structures, but to my mind Nicholas Freeling describes it well in one of his good Dutch thrillers as "a rather nasty *art nouveau* building which replaced a neo-classical horror. There is a popular Amsterdamse myth that there is a huge crack in the wall. Occasionally the city fathers are disposed to believe in this myth, but they have never had enough courage to knock the huge block down." In the Jewish quarter, five thousand deserted houses were torn apart for firewood in the last desperate winter of the war, and later knocked down; but this part of the city is still full of devastated sites. Here and there the rubble has been replaced by a well-designed children's playground, but the general state seems to be one of blitzed suspension—in fact, waiting for the construction of the first Amsterdam Metro line. This will speed commuters in from the new Bijlmermeer development (which is too far out for bicycles), making a necessary connection between the offices, shops, and entertainments of the city center with the people who no longer live very close to it. The Metro, however, also bothers people. Some think it is too grandiose a conception (the Bijlmermeer line being only the first of the proposed, extensive system). Some suggest that the construction will unsettle many historic buildings, for the sand waves under the city react uneasily to any pressure. When the C & A department store was built on the Damrak a nearby church settled eight millimeters. When the water level in the Vondelpark was changed, several houses on the park borders had to be re-piled at great expense—and the word "re-pile" sends shudders through every Amsterdam householder, describing as it does a fate far worse than rising damp or termites. Some suggest connecting a Metro from the suburbs with a less destructive high-speed water-tram, which would run around the canals of the old city.

The Bijlmermeer is an aspect of the Amsterdam situation that can be profitably dwelt on. Because many people have moved to suburban towns and to new developments, of which the Bijlmermeer is the most recent, Amsterdam is less densely populated than it used to be. Although it has extended its urban boundaries, the total population is down from 872,000 in 1958 to 866,000 in 1965. This outward movement has of course taken place in most big Western cities, but here in Amsterdam the new developments give the impression of being collections of great sponges, designed to sop up the outgoing tide of people. They remind some Dutchmen, in fact, of dikes; the planners perhaps are doing what the dike-builders used to do, in the latter case holding back the sea and in the former holding back a sea of people. J. H. Huizinga, a newspaper columnist, writes: "It is as if the planners have been as much concerned to protect what remains of the countryside as to provide new housing." Certainly some of the old and new sections of Amsterdam haven't been well blended or connected. In the Slotervaart section such a connection was attempted by flooding a large area to make a lake but, as R. Blijstra points out, the lake is a bit too big and doesn't do much to help establish a feeling of coherence between the developments and the city. And the developments themselves to my mind perhaps express the planners' distaste for the crowded, grubby conditions which obtain in some old sections of Amsterdam, in the nineteenth-century tenements around the Kinkerstraat or the Dapperstraat, for example, rather than the denser, more varied (and also more up-to-date) conditions those people, moving out, might enjoy. About the Bijlmermeer, with its parking garages, its mammoth apartment blocks which seem, in plan, to take the shape of giant question marks, its elevated motorways and areas of park, and its complete absence of Dutch coziness, one is tempted to think that although it may be of higher quality, as construction, than the earlier developments, yet it is still the kind of building that municipal authorities put up for "other people." The planners and architects would probably rather not live in them. (I believe it is only Bulgaria that has the enlightened rule demanding that architects live at least a year in any apartment building they design.) Yet the height of these buildings is, except for the family with small children, not a bad thing. Eight stories gives you a superb view over the Dutch countryside, and I imagine that most Dutchmen appreciate being so high above sea level.

In any event, time, which darkens things, may produce reasons for feeling affection for the Bijlmermeer. Certainly, a comparison with any New York metropolitan equivalent like Co-op City reflects favorably on the Dutch development. And just as the Amsterdam "cupboard dwellings" (hurriedly constructed with the prosperity brought by the completion of the North Sea Canal in 1874) have come to seem, despite their eight flats and one toilet, quite cheerful dwellings, so the Bijlmermeer apartments may yet take on a touch or two of home. The Amsterdam authorities are ashamed of their nineteenth-century dilapidated sections, with houses (as in the Dapperstraat) whose poor exterior condition now reflects the owner's knowledge that they will be pulled down in the next ten years or so. However, judged by the standards of a Harlem, New York City, tenement or a North of England slum, these buildings are by no means dreadful. Many people who live in them, at miniscule rents, have made comfortable homes within the shabby shells. The Kinkerstraat is a lively, inexpensive shopping street, and the Dapperstraat every day contains a bustling street market, where you can buy cheaply almost anything you need—a pair of socks, a piece of fish, a sack of potatoes, a secondhand coat, or a battery for your car. The barrows and stalls line the broad street in opposing ranks; cars are unwelcome; and people not only of the shabby neighborhood but of more affluent sections of town promenade through the market, reconnoitering the merchandise for the best goods at the best prices, and exchanging banter with the street merchants. Amsterdam has its own vulgar, earthy humor, which flourishes in such places as the Dapperstraat, and will not, I imagine, last long in such sections as the Bijlmermeer. Certainly in the daily market it is easy to understand the concern that the more imaginative Dutch architects have with the *street*—what Constant Nieuwenhuys calls "social space," which is to be found in the courtyards of old *hofjes*, the covered street of Het Dorp, the broad corridors of Aldo van Eyck's children's home, and the arcade and staircases of Herman Hertzberger's students' hostel in the Weesperstraat.

I had a drink one afternoon with Hertzberger on the terrace café of the Schiller Hotel in the Rembrandtsplein. This square is the Broadway of Amsterdam, with nightclubs, restaurants, and cinemas, and it is full of a Manhattan kind of hustle; trams, cars, and bicycles whizz past the inept nineteenth-century statue of Rembrandt, and noise and dust rise from the expansion work being done on the offices of the Amro Bank. Hertzberger is a stocky man of thirty-six, with a shock of black wavy hair and surprised eyebrows. On this occasion he wore a black leather jacket and a tartan shirt and washed down an occasional aspirin with tonic water as he spoke, in a slightly French-flavored English, and with a kind of friendly impatience, about the city.

"Amsterdam is a fantastic responsibility—it is one of the three best-preserved large old cities in the world, and so much of it seems much better than anything we are capable of making now. It is also a bit of a drawback from a planning point of view—the old buildings and the

old pattern impose restrictions on our freedom. Yet it
also makes important demands. It obliges us to make sure
the center doesn't become a ghetto of banks and offices.
It asks for more of the university, more shops, more
schools, more people living in it and being in it. Fortunately, some of the big offices are beginning to move out
to the edge of the city—the textile industry is doing this,
for one—and this is making a difference in terms of cars
and trucks in the center. This problem of the new Metro
could be alleviated by giving the dormitory towns
around the city hearts of their own—then so many people wouldn't want to come into the center and the Metro
wouldn't need to be so big."

He took another sip of tonic water. "We are Dutch—
sometimes too Dutch. Look at Mondrian—so consistent,
so *puritan*. Somewhere in the Bible it says something
like 'There are no poles—meaning no fences or divisions
—in the realm of God.' Well, in one part of Holland this
saying, taken literally, has prevented them from ever
having telephone poles, and hence telephones. Then
there's the story about Emperor Charles V at a banquet
in Brussels. He asked who were the men in the corner
who hadn't doffed their hats. 'Ah, sire, those are the
Dutch.' We can be hopelessly stiff-necked and rigid. For
the past generation we have been artificially separating
all the elements of new communities—work, play, shopping, sleeping. That was the way it had to be. In the
same way, once we'd thought of a Metro, fifty years
after everyone else, it simply had to be built. And yet
here we are living in these swamps. Who else would

have lived here? It's quite ridiculous. And so we have adapted to these absurd conditions. We have become tenacious. We have become well organized. Now we have to learn how to be flexible—how, for instance, to construct these large system-built apartment blocks and retain within them a freedom, a sense of possibility, so that the dining table in every flat isn't in the same place for the next hundred years. Rooms must allow for different uses. A house should be a framework within which people can do what they want—not a frame in which a collective pattern is imposed on them."

From where we sat we could see Rembrandt's bronze back. People walking past looked at all the people sitting in the sidewalk café, and the people on the terrace stared at the people walking by, with that particular stare the Dutch have, which seems at once to see and not to see. I told Hertzberger I admired his student hostel in the Weesperstraat.

He said: "Choice and communication are what count in a city. A crowd doesn't matter if you have the communications to match the growing crowdedness. A town is possibility. A town—or a city, or whatever you want to call this dense, urban world—is talk, the possibility of people exchanging ideas and feelings. It works if it allows this. If it doesn't, then you're in trouble. So that's part of what I had in mind in the Weesperstraat hostel, and also in a new Montessori school I've designed in Delft. There, in the main entrance hallway, I put this big wooden block, about five feet square and two feet high. It has no real form and no obvious function. And yet it works marvelously well. Visitors stop there and put down their briefcases while they take their coats off. The headmaster has started climbing up on it and making speeches. Children use it for all sorts of things—to leave their musical instruments on, or sit on to read and draw during the lunch hour. Children play games round it. Small children stand on it and become taller. Teachers stand up on it to explain things. It is a stage, a resting place, a meeting place, a playground. It is a touchstone. People are unintentionally drawn to it and talk to one another. It is, in a way, a city."

⚘ **22** ⚘

AMONG THE POSSIBILITIES of Amsterdam I have some favorites: the print cabinet of the Rijksmuseum, where scholars brood over the etchings of Hercules Seghers or the drawings of Rembrandt, hypnotized by a squiggle of ink or the burred stroke of the needle; the sculpture garden of the Stedelijk Museum, which can be entered without going through the museum building—entered, in other words, for free—and where you can sit out of the Dutch wind to eat a lunchtime sandwich, seeing the Baroque cornices of the Concertgebouw over the shaggy hedges, and within, against a background of small trees and tall bronze and concrete forms, children playing in the sandpit (it is, by the way, an excellent sandpit, with a six-inch-broad, one-foot-high concrete lip, good for sitting on, wheeling toys around, rolling over, or jumping off); and of course the Kalverstraat, the fashionable and justly famous shopping street which is devoted to walkers. It is interesting that the Kalverstraat, known as one of the earliest pedestrian malls, has in fact become so over forty years by use rather than by law. Access to it for cars on the narrow side streets is difficult; entrance to the streets is camouflaged or unwelcoming. The Kalverstraat itself is for a few blocks one-way southbound and then becomes one-way northbound and so on, alternating for its entire length in a series of what for cars are cul-de-sacs, but for walkers is a continuous traffic-free street into which only the most urgent and most knowledgeable delivery vehicles attempt to enter. Drivers are so inhibited that most don't know that the Kalverstraat may be freely parked in every evening after 7 P.M.

In much of Holland you have the feeling that the last of Dutch sex life went to invigorate the paintings of Jan Steen. Walking in Amsterdam you realize that Dutch interest in this matter, in every highly colored hue and variation, has come to nest here, in gay bars, transvestite night clubs, or the more orthodox though no less strident taverns along the Zeedijk. Here and in the surrounding streets that back upon the Oudezijds Voorburgwal, walking and window-shopping have novel dimensions. In little downstairs rooms the women sit like tulips in their picture windows or, rather, like still-lives, like the arrange-

ments of things that are so dear to every Dutchman's
heart. Perhaps it is partly the presence in the area of old
spice warehouses, but there is hereabouts what the French
author Bernard Pingaud calls "a faint odor of corrup-
tion." The tender nuance of flesh lends to the city a
character similar to that given by Indonesian flavors to
Dutch food; what was open and straightforward is now
more subtle and mysterious, what was flat has some kick
in it. Now, many of the girls in this section are Indonesian. They stand in basement doorways as well as in
windows, and smile and wave rather than simply sit and
comb their hair. Toward the New Babylon!

My slight feeling of optimism about the Bijlmermeer
and the other Amsterdam dormitory developments is perhaps supported by the "New South" section of the city,
built in the 1920's and 1930's following the plans of
Berlage. The five-story apartment buildings built in continuous rows on monumentally laid-out avenues and
streets are at first sight dull and heavy. But ivy has
grown on them. Children, here as elsewhere, play in the
streets or on the grass strips of the boulevards. There is
a sense of neighborhoods that have welled up within the
plans—on the Beethovenstraat, for instance, where small
family hotels lurk in the upstairs floors above the shops,
and delicatessens and tobacconists provide not only
goods but gossip. Here too, as in Holland everywhere, it
seems to be unimportant that the elements themselves
be beautiful if the total arrangement, the whole of which
they are parts, is lively and various and cared for.

When I was walking one day it struck me that the

Dutch do not need to build an urban model counterpart
to the hydraulics models in the laboratory at Delft:
Amsterdam is such a model for them. The city is a communal work of art providing the key to the country as a
work of art. I didn't have any rose-colored glasses on at
the time, but I had come to one of Amsterdam's six hundred and thirty-five bridges, not one of which is quite
the same as another, and was watching things pass:
ducks, leaves floating on their own reflections, glass-
topped *rondvaart* boots full of tourists, and the occasional
abandoned wooden shoe. Water is a basis of the communication Amsterdam encourages; water moves. Over
the bridge, I walked along the canal bank until I came to
a wider waterway, and it was a moment before I realized
it wasn't just another and bigger canal, it was the Amstel
River. Perhaps because of the prevalence of water in the
city, the Amstel seems a little less to Amsterdam than
what the Seine is to Paris or the Thames to London, but
it is in fact the stem and core of the apple which is
Amsterdam. It takes a long, broad sweep from the
Heerengracht to Korte Ouderkerkerdijk, past the Amstel-
hof, the Six house, the open sluices built in 1674 and
once used to regulate the water level of the city canals,
past the Theater Carré, the Amstel Hotel (which is
Amsterdam's best), and the former Stalinlaan Bridge—
since renamed Vrijheidslaan. (Churchillaan and Roose-
veltlaan remain, but Stalin has been changed to Freedom.) Medium-sized cargo barges move along the
Amstel, and moored along the banks are barges of all
kinds, some derelict, some being made into floating

homes by do-it-yourself craftsmen, and a few that have
become the shelters of emigrés, like the Henry David
Thoreau, an ancient black sailing barge which is now the
home of the "New Amsterdam School of Ikon Painting."

Where the three aristocratic seventeenth-century canals
swing north on the eastern side of the Amstel and come
to an end at the Plantage Middenlaan is Artis, the zoo.
Artis seems a funny sort of name until you know that the
motto of the hundred-year-old zoological garden and
aquarium is *Natura Artis Magistra* ("Nature Is the
Teacher of ,Art"), and out of this the people of Amsterdam have abstracted the one word *Artis* by which to call
their zoo. Artis was built in the gardens of the former
Plantage—a smaller and less rural Amsterdamse Bos or
green belt of times past, where there were summer
houses a little like those in the allotments today. A few
of these cottages and formal paths remain among the
bear pits and lion dens. The zoo is bigger than the
menagerie in New York's Central Park and smaller than
the zoo in London's Regent's Park; it has a cozy but
not crowded feeling. The monkeys are cheerful and the
penguins rock contentedly back and forth upon their
heels. No animals seem to be having fits. Artis boasts a
splendid record of wild animals born in captivity, and
the Amsterdammers stroll through looking at the young
camels, baby hippos, and infant dugongs who testify so
vitally to good Dutch care.

Many evenings while we lived at Schellingwoude, a
dike village on the northeastern boundary of Amsterdam,
I would walk along the Schellingwoudedijk to the

Oranjesluis, the set of locks between Amsterdam harbor and the IJsselmeer. Each of the three adjacent locks is roughly a hundred yards long, and in the evenings around six o'clock there was always a lot of traffic going through—boats and barges trying to ensure that they were on the right side of the locks for an early start next morning. Although four or five lockkeepers would be busily on duty then, spectators were tolerated; there were generally three or four small boys with fishing rods, and three or four old men with fishing rods and cigars. People walking or cycling home from Amsterdam-East to Schellingwoude would pause for a minute in the course of making their way around the lock gates (which had railed catwalks for pedestrians to cross on) and watch what was happening. Now and then one of the spectators would take a line from a barge as it slid into the lock, or would stoop to flip a warp off a lockside bollard for a barge getting underway, but most stood back out of the way against a railing and enjoyed the activity.

One soon realized that the lockkeepers took pride in fitting as many craft as possible in a single lock. They didn't want to waste a drop of water—the greater the cubic footage or volume of water displaced by boats and barges, the less was needed in the lock. Moreover, they didn't want to waste the energy involved in opening and shutting the lock gates more often than was necessary; this was done by cranking gears by hand. But though this was the general preoccupation, one of the lockkeepers had brought it to full flower. He was the tight-fit champion of the Oranjesluis. I watched him at work one evening, first summoning in by loud-hailer a big Rhine oil barge, which at a distance looked as if it would fill the entire lock. It was a barge with a professional deck-hand as well as the skipper and his family, and carried not only the usual deck-top accouterments such as play-pen and bicycles but a new Fiat sedan and a motor-cycle, with gangplanks for running them ashore when the barge docked at a suitable wharf. The barge was so long the skipper had an intercom for communicating with the foredeck hand, and we could hear a few brief commands coming over this system as he brought the barge into the lock and made a faultless mooring, first snubbing in the bow and then, when the bow lines were made fast, swinging in the stern to the lockside.

There was still some room beside this leviathan, and the lockkeeper had already ordered in several slightly smaller craft, which now made their approach. First a medium-sized cargo barge with the skipper on the fore-deck bellowing back to his wife, a plump, aproned lady who stood spinning the big wheel while the baby attempted to climb over the side of its crib and the ragout bubbled on the gas-cooker behind her. She looked absolutely unruffled, but she didn't have the requisite expertise in this instance. There was a bang, harmless but loud enough, as the barge's bow caromed off the wooden fender along the lockside. Sparks flew as the skipper threw the loop of a wire warp over the iron bol-lard and quickly made it fast to the bitts on the barge. That done, ignoring the skipper of the big Rhine barge who, equally aloof, stood coiling a stern line almost above his head, he cast a baleful look back at the plump figure in the pilot-house, now spinning the wheel the other way. Next to come in was an Amsterdam-Marken tourist boat, listing rather heavily to starboard as all the passengers ran to one side to look at the barges. Three yachts were then brought in—one German, one Dutch, and one English—and arranged, not without a certain amount of bumping and apprehensive trilingual shouting, in the narrow gap between the barges and the tourist boat. There was still room, the lockmaster decided, for a tug, towing a broken-down North Sea fishing boat, and after that had been made fast, slightly askew across the lock, and we were all expecting him to close the gates and lower the water to ‚Amsterdam level, he took a quick look and waved in three Belgian coastal patrol boats, manned by sea cadets. These boats had been hovering in an excited, unsure manner off the lock entrance, rather than being tied up properly at the staging where boats waited in order of arrival. Now, when the first patrol boat got to where the commander could see the crowded conditions in the lock, he threw his engine into reverse and stopped—surely he wasn't expected to go in there? But the lockkeeper shouted and waved him in. Meanwhile other officials on the lock were getting the tug to snub the fishing boat in closer. The English yacht was ordered to rearrange itself closer to the German. On the small barge they swung in their steel skiff on its davit to prevent it bumping the bow of the tourist boat. On the big barge the deckhand had a word with the skipper and hung out several fenders over the barge's unprotected flank. Then, with a good deal of friendly advice from the men on the tug, the young Belgians made their nervous entry.

When they had their lines made fast you could hardly see the surface of the water in the lock. The lockmaster gave the assembled craft a casual glance and went to the gates to shut them. And then there was a period of quiet, lasting ten minutes or so, while the water level in the lock fell from that of the IJsselmeer to that of Amsterdam harbor. The deckhand on the big barge got out some grey paint and touched up a few chips. The skipper's wife on the smaller barge fed the baby some ragout. One of the crew members of the tug made a quick dash into Schellingwoude to buy a loaf of bread. The youngsters on the lockside continued to fish and the old men chewed on their pipes and the passengers on the tourist boat gazed out over the masts and decks toward the spiry and towered skyline of the city. It seemed to me that perhaps for some time I had been wandering around in search of a place that assembled many of the things that make Holland impressive; and here it was—a place where the rules were strict, the elements were put to work and respected, very little was wasted, and people found themselves in a tight and not uncomradely fit; there was even hospitable room for people from elsewhere. But I didn't linger on this thought. The lockmaster and a colleague were at the other gates, the gates were opening, and the members of that motley fleet untangled themselves and sailed on.

Author's Note

Two books have been particularly useful to me: Sir William Temple's *Observations upon the United Provinces of the Netherlands*, first published in 1673; and Bernard Pingaud's *Holland*, a small paperback (New York: Viking Press, 1962). I have also found instructive:

The Making of Dutch Towns (1956), and *Greenheart Metropolis* (1966), both by Gerald L. Burke and published by Macmillan and Co., London.

Dutch Society, by Johan Goudsblom (New York: Random House, 1967)

Ashes in the Wind, by Dr. J. Presser (New York: E. P. Dutton, 1966)

The Dutch Puzzle, by the Duke de Baena (The Hague: Boucher, 1967)

Those Dutch Catholics, by M. van der Plas and H. Suèr (New York: Macmillan Co., 1968)

Homo Ludens, by Johan Huizinga (Boston: Beacon Press, 1955)

The Dutch under German Occupation, by W. Warmbrunn (Stanford: Stanford University Press, 1963)

Town Planning in the Netherlands since 1900, by R.

Blijstra (Amsterdam: P. N. Kampen & Zoon, N.V., no date)

Indonesia, by Bruce Grant (Baltimore: Penguin, 1967)

The Herring Gull's World, by Niko Tinbergen (Garden City, N.Y.: Doubleday Anchor Book, 1967)

Daily Life in Rembrandt's Holland, by Paul Zumthor (New York: Macmillan and Co., 1963)

Dredge, Drain, Reclaim, by Johan van Veen (The Hague: Trio, n.d.)

Several pieces in the English magazine *New Society* have given me facts and ideas, and many articles in *Delta*, a quarterly review of Dutch art, life, and thought, have done so too. Most statistics and figures come from the *Statistisch Zakboek* of 1967, official government digests, and ministerial reports of 1967 and 1968, and from a booklet, *The Netherlands—Work and Prosperity* (second edition, 1967). Photographs were generously provided by the Netherlands Rijkswaterstaat, Amsterdam Dept. of Public Works, Netherlands Information Service, City of Amsterdam Press Office, City of Rotterdam Information Dept., the Municipality of Drachten, Ab van Dien, and Dick van der Zee. I was greatly helped by conversations with Dr. Arie Querido, Dr. Fiedeldij Dop, Ian McHarg, Miss Hofman, Miss Hoeflake, and many Dutchmen including Messrs Dam, Gerritzen, Blom, Brandsma, Wolf, van Soest, van den Eyck, de Lange, Brouwer, Bos, Hertzberger, Pennink, Plemper, van der Palm, van Chagen, Klunder, Wegener-Sleeswijk, de Zoeten, van Kerkwijk, van Dien, Hoog, van Kuyk, Smits,

Author's Note

Lindenbergh, Adema, Heuvelman, Rey, Froger, van Esterik, Tenhaeff, and van der Zee. I was glad to have the assistance of the librarian of the Netherlands Press Museum, and for the kindness of many Dutch families, among them the Hamakers, the Beijderwellens, the de Goejes, the Vonkemans, and the Heermas. And most of all, I am grateful for the friendship of Jon and Marianne Swan.

Index

Aalsmeer, 134
Adema, Mr., 209–13
Adrian VI, 180
Afsluitdyk, 94, 106
aged, care of, 213–19
agriculture, 88, 118–19, 132, 135,
  145–53
Alfrink, Cardinal, 180
allotment land, 137–8
almshouses, 214–19
Amersfoort, 73
Amstelveem, 134
Amsterdam, 15, 18–19, 25–6, 28,
  47, 52, 65–7, 69, 70–1, 79–80,
  84, 89–90, 92, 114, 132–8, 201–2,
  203, 214–15, 217–19, 229–59
Amsterdam City Council, 232,
  236, 239
Amsterdam Stock Exchange, 244
Amsterdam Zoological Society, 156
Amsterdam-Rotterdam Bank, 71
Amsterdamse Bos, 132–6
Antwerp, 241
A.N.W.B., 176
architecture, 17–27, 33–4, 65, 66,
  75–80, 113–15, 120–1, 209–12,
  219–20, 237–8, 243 ff.
Arnhem, 208
art and artists, 8, 52–4, 80–2, 205,
  213, 254–5
Artis, 156, 255
aviation, 29–30, 33, 39, 135

Bakker, Jacob, 210
Banning, Willem, 177

Bas, Tabe, 189
Beatrix, Princess, 197, 231–2
Begijnhof, 214–15
Bekkers, Bishop Wilhelmus, 180–1
Bergen-op-zoom, 65
Berger, John, 81
Berlage, 244
Bernhard, Prince, 55–6
bicycles and bicycling, 6, 10–11, 30,
  51–2, 232–3
Bijlmermeer, 244–8
Blaman, Anna, 41
Blau, Joseph L., 38
Blijstra, R., 120–1, 246
Blom, Ivo, 36, 110–12, 115, 227
Boeklo, 89
Bos, S. G., 92, 93
Bos (The Hague), 132
Bosch, Hieronymus, 48
Boswell, James, 8, 187
Botlek, 110
Brandsma, Menno, 123–5, 175–6,
  225
Breughel II, Jan, 140
Brouwershavengat, 104–6
Buitenveldert, 33
"Bull, The" (Potter), 146
Burke, Gerald L., 21, 66

Calvinism, 172–9 *passim,* 201
camping, 126–30
Camus, Albert, 169
Carolus (Blaman), 41
Carus, C. G., 59
Catholicism, 172–86

Index

charity, 203 *ff.*
Charles V, 249
children, 24–9, 208–13
C.I.A.M., 25–6, 120–1
class structure, 175
claustrophobia, 35–6
cleanliness, 28, 43–5
Cleveringa, R. P., 200
Coleridge, Samuel, 90–1
Colijnsplaat, 97
colonialism, 190–1
Concordia Hotel, 99
Constant (Nieuwenhuys), 126–7, 237–8, 248
cosmopolitanism, 188–90
Couperus, Louis, 35–6, 41, 190
Cremer, Jan, 48
crime, 46, 47
Croiset, Gérard, 56, 58

d'Ailly, A. J., 236
dairy farming, 145–53
Dalrymple, David, 8
Dapperstraat (Amsterdam), 18–19, 246, 247–8
de Baena, Duke, 39, 45, 196–7
de Genestet, P. H., 64
de Lange, Mr., 197
De Stijl: *see* Stijl, De
de Vries, A. B., 53–4
de Vries, Bernhard, 243
de Zoeten, Willem, 206
Delft, 30–5, 94–5, 101, 200
Delta plan, 95 *ff.*
Descartes, 187
diamond trade, 203, 241
Dieuw, Tante, 202
dikes and canals, 64 *ff.*, 89–90, 94 *ff.*, 121 *ff.*, 242 *ff.*, 255–9
divorce, 38
Dokkum, 90, 158
Donner, Jan Hein, 177, 230
Dop, H. Fiedeldy, 25–7, 76
Dorp, Het, 208–13, 248

drinking, 46, 83, 115–16, 170
Drion, Huibert, 222
Dronten, 175–6
Duinlandschap (van de Velde), 85–6
dunes, 84–8, 92–4, 104, 126–30
Dutch Society (Goudsblom), 40

East Flevoland, 119
education, 42–3, 174–6, 187
Eindhoven, 35, 73, 183
Einstein, Albert, 187
Emmeloord, 174
Enkhuisen, 214
Enschede Printers, 32, 82–3
Europoort, 109–18 *passim*, 238

Fall, The (Camus), 169
family relationships, 24–8, 37–41
Farmer's Party, 234–5
Flakkee, 97
Flevoland, 114, 119 *ff.*
flooding, 96
Forest Service, 131
Fortman, Dr. W. F. de Gaay, 221, 224–5
Frank, Anne, 197, 232
Frederick of Bohemia, 187
Freeling, Nicholas, 244
Freud, Sigmund, 187
Friesland, 146–52, 202–3, 220
Frisian lakes, 126
furnishings, 6, 8–10, 41 *ff.*, 76 *ff.*

gardening, 36, 137–45
Garonne, Monsignor, 184
Geiger, Theodore, 223
Gelderland, 81–2, 126, 130
geography, 63–7, 94 *ff.*
Germans, relations with, 195–203, 232

Index

Gerritzen, K. J. M., 99–106 *passim*

Geuzenveld, 65–6

"Girl Reading a Letter" (Vermeer), 53

Goddijn, Father Walter, 183

Goerdereede, 101

Gouda, 83

Goudsblom, J., 40, 173, 223

government-in-exile, 198–200

Grant, Bruce, 190

Groningen, 30, 35, 73, 146

Grootveld, Robert Jasper, 230–1, 236

Grotius, 187

Haanstra, Bert, 116

Haarlem, 8, 32, 36, 82–3, 132, 142–5, 188, 215–19, 228–9

Haarlemmer Hout park, 131

Hague, The, 5, 15, 80, 82, 92, 132, 138

Hall, Peter, 72–3

handicapped, community for, 208

Haringvliet, 100 *ff*.

Harmsen, Ger, 235

healers, 55–6

health, 24–5, 46, 89, 90, 207 *ff*.

Heerma, Enneus, and family, 146–52, 155, 179, 202–3, 234–5

Heine, Heinrich, 3–4

Hepworth, Barbara, 82

Hermans, Willem, 41

Hertogenbosch, 's-: *see* 's-Hertogenbosch

Hertzberger, Herman, 76, 219, 248–51

Heuvelaken, 76–9

Heuvelman, Mr., 133–6

Hofmans, Greet, 55–6

Holford, William, 70

Homo Ludens (Huizinga), 238–9

Hoog, Thomas, 36, 142–5, 215–17

Hooge Veluwe, the, 81–2, 118, 130–1

Hoorn, 202

hostel, student, 219–20, 248, 250–1

housing, 17–27, 33–4, 75–80, 114–15, 209–12, 213 *ff*., 237–8

Housing Act (1901), 70

Hudson, Henry, 241

Huguenots, 188

Huizinga, J. H., 245–6

Huizinga, Johan, 69, 119, 238–9

IJ, 240

IJmuiden, 89

IJsselmeer, 89, 94, 118, 126

immigration, 189–90

Indonesia (Grant), 190

Indonesians, 190–4

industrial relations, 220–5

industries, 72–3

Institute for Applied Scientific Research, 31–5

International Commission for the Protection against Pollution of the river Rhine, 91

introversion, 50 *ff*.

Ishwaran, K., 37

Ivens, Joris, 116, 187

Jewish Council, 201

Jews, 174, 188, 197–203, 221

Johnson, Paul, 184

Juliana, Queen, 56, 192

Kampen, 123

Katwijk an Zee, 10–11, 17–18, 23–24, 28, 48, 84 *ff*., 95–6, 118, 174, 194, 196, 204, 208, 214, 228

Katwijk aan Rijn, 174

Ketchum, Morris, 114

Keukenhof, 141–2

Kinkerstraat (Amsterdam), 246, 247

Index

Klunder, Herman, 79–80
Koster, Koosje, 232
Krauweel, Dr. Henry, 205
Kroller-Muller Museum, 81–2, 130

labor, 180, 189, 220–5, 238
Labor, Foundation of, 223
landscape, 63–4
Last, Jef, 230
Leeuwarden, 45, 65, 145, 220
Leeuwenhoek, Anton van, 5
Leiden, 65, 187, 188, 215
Leiden University, 200
Lely, Cornelius, 118
Lelystad, 114, 120
Leyster, Judith, 139, 144
Lieverdje, Het, 230–1
Lijnbaan (Rotterdam), 114, 115
literature, 35–6, 40–1, 48
litter, 44–5
"littleness," 4–14
Lunteren, 126, 130, 131, 194, 205–6
Lutherans, 174, 181

Maasvlakte, 110
Maduro, George, 12
Madurodam, 11–14
Making of Dutch Towns, The (Burke), 66
Maliepaard, C. H. J., 131
Manifesto of 1917, 80
Maria Christina, Princess, 55
Mauritshuis (The Hague), 146
mental health, 24–7, 45–9, 207–8
Mesmerism, 55
Metro, 244–5, 249
Middelburg, 65, 98
Mondrian, 80, 249
Montessori, Madame, 187
motorcycles, 30–1
Mulisch, Harry, 236

Nagele, 114, 120–1
Netherlands Bank building, 243–4
New Amsterdam School of Ikon Painting, 255
New Waterway, 101, 110, 112, 117–18
New Ways of Living, 25, 76–80, 217
newspapers, 174
Nieuwenhuys, Constant, 126–7, 237–8, 248
"Night Watch, The" (Rembrandt), 8, 53, 83–4
noise, 29–35
Nordholt, Professor, 227
North Holland, 69, 92
North Sea Canal, 247

Old People and the Things That Pass (Couperus), 35–6, 41, 190
Oldeboorn, 146–52, 155–6, 203
Oosterhout, 116–17
Oostmahoorn, 45
orphanage, 208–13, 248
Osdorp, 20–1, 22–3, 65–6
Ottaviani, Cardinal, 180, 185
Otterloo, 81–2
Oud, J. P., 80
Ouderkerk, 97, 98
Overijssel, 82

paragnosts, 54–9
Parapsychology Institute, 54, 58
Pardoel, Mr., 115–16
Parival, Jean-Nicholas, 28–9
parks, wooded, 81–2, 103–6
Parool, Het, 200
Pastoral Council, 185
Paul, Pope, 185
Pendrecht, 20, 25, 114–15
Philips, 35
Physical Planning Act (1965), 71–2

Index

Pieterburen, 158–65
Pilgrims, 188
Pingaud, Bernard, 188
planning, 20–2, 25–6, 66–7, 68 *ff.*, 109 *ff.*, 118 *ff.*, 132 *ff.*
Plemper, Mr., 218
political groupings, 180
pollution, 90–2, 117–18
Poppen, Jacob, 188
Popta, Dr., 220
population, 3 *ff.*, 14–16, 72, 241, 245
port facilities, 109–18 *passim*
Potter, Paul, 146
Presser, Dr. Jacob, 202
printing, 32, 82–3
Prinz Alexander Polder, 20–1
privacy, 21–4, 26–7
prostitution, 39
Provo, 43, 81, 230–9
Provo (paper), 234, 236
psychotherapy, 54–5

Querido, Dr. Arie, 21–2, 25, 36, 44, 46–7, 50, 68, 70, 171–2

Raadhuis (Veere), 108
Randstad, 5 *ff.*, 14 *ff.*, 30, 38, 67, 72–3, 131 *ff.*
Rasmussen, Steen, 65
reclamation, 63–7, 73, 82, 94 *ff.*, 118 *ff.*
recreation, 12–14, 50, 84 *ff.*, 126–39, 153–65, 238–9
Red Cross associations, 173, 200
refugees, 186–92
religion, 172–86, 201
Rembrandt, 8, 10, 51, 83–4, 241
Rembrandtsplein (Amsterdam), 248 *ff.*
Research Institute for Public Health Engineering, 31–5
resistance, World War II, 198 *ff.*
Rhine River and delta, 15, 90–3

Rietveld, Gerrit, 80–1, 116
Rijksmuseum, 52–4, 85–6, 251
Rijnland Waterschaap, 144–5
Rijnmond, 117
Rockanje, 110
Rotterdam, 5, 6, 15, 20–1, 69, 71, 79–80, 91, 109–18, 138, 198, 202
Rotterdam-Vlissingen highway, 101
Ruhr, 15, 196

sailing, 154–7
St. Bavo's Church (Haarlem), 8, 228–9
salt, 88–9, 93
Sassenheim, 179
Scaliger, 187
Scheldt River and delta, 15, 95 *ff.*, 241
Schellingwoude, 255–9
Schiermonnikoog, 127–30, 157–8
Schilderboek (Van Mander), 48
Schillebeeckx, Edward, 182–3
Schimmelpenninck, Lund, 230, 236
Schiphol, 29–30, 33, 135
Second Physical Planning Report, 74
sectarianism, 172–5
Seghers, Hercules, 153
sewage, 89 *ff.*
's-Hertogenbosch, 48
shipping, 109–18 *passim*, 256–9
Sick Fund, 207
slaves, 188
Slotermeer, 65–6
Slotervaart, 20–1, 65–6, 246
Smith, G. E. Kidder, 75
Social Affairs, Ministry of, 207
Social and Economic Council, 223
social consciousness, 203–20
social structure, 37 *ff.*, 169 *ff.*
Socialism, 180, 222
South Holland, 69
Spade, Law of the, 65
Spinoza, 187

Index

Staphorst, 177–8
Stedelijk Museum, 251–2
Steigenga, Willem, 75
Stellendam, 101
Stieltjes, Thomas, 189
Stijl, De, 80–2
Suèr, Henk, 184
Surhuisterveen, 178–9

T.N.O. (Dutch Institute for Applied Scientific Research), 31–5
teenagers, 194
television, 27, 47–8, 176, 177, 188–9
Temple, Sir William, 43–4, 75, 83, 157, 187, 203–4, 214, 222, 241–2
Tenhaeff, W. H. C., 54–9
Thijsse, Jac. P., 69
Tinbergen, Niko, 86
tolerance, 186–94, 195 ff.
tourism, 195–7
town planning, 20–2, 25–6, 66–7, 68 ff., 109 ff., 119 ff., 137–8, 208, 237–8, 242 ff.
Town-planning in the Netherlands since 1900 (Blijstra), 121
trade unionism, 180, 221–5
traditionalism, 177–8
traffic, 6–7, 10–11, 51–2, 226–7, 232–4, 242 ff.
travel, 50
tulips, 139–45
Tulp, Nicholas, 204

universities, 187
Utrecht, 30, 54, 187, 188
Utrecht, State University of, 56

van de Velde, Elias, 85–6
van den Eijk, J., 31–4
van der Plas, Michel, 184

van der Zee, Dick, 159–65
van Dien, Ab, 76
van Doesburg, Theo, 80, 81
van Duyn, Roel, 235
van Eyck, Aldo, 76, 210–12, 219, 236, 248
van Hall, Gijsbert, 232, 234
van Heeckeren van Molecaten, Baron, 55, 56
van Hees, Nico, 180
van Heutsz, General, 231
van Lennop, Carl, 229–30
van Mander, Carel, 48
van Rooijen, Professor, 227
van Schendel, Arthur, 41
van Soest, Mr., 197
van Veen, Dr. J., 64
van Wetering, Irene, 230, 233
Veere, 107–9
Veersegat, 107
Veluwe: see Hooge Veluwe
Verhoeven, Jan, 78
Vermeer, Jan, 53–4
Vermooten, W. H., 138
Vink, J., 72
vital statistics, 15–16, 46
Vlaardingen, 117
Volendam, 201
von Amsberg, Claus, 197, 231–2
Vondelpark, the, 245
Vonkeman, Mr. and Mrs. Martin, 128–30, 205–6
Voorne, 116–17
Vrijburg, Father Jos, 184

Waddenzee, 157–65
walking (*wadlopen*), 157–65
Wallon, Hospice, 218–19
Wappen van Huizingoo Inn, 159
Wassenaar, 86
water supply, 88–94, 95
Waterman, The (Van Schendel), 41
welfare, 203–19

Index

Westersingel, 90
Westland, 116–17
Wierum, 147
wildlife, 86–7, 93–4, 122–4, 132 ff.,
  156–7
Wilhelm, Kaiser, 187
Wilhelmina, Queen, 56, 148, 198,
  217, 222–3
wind, 67, 154
woods, park, 81–2, 130–6
Woods, the, 132–6
World Cities (Hall), 72–3

World War II, 121, 148, 195–203,
  206, 207, 221
Wright, Frank Lloyd, 79

yachting, 154–7, 258–9
Yerseke, 69

Zeeland, 98–109, 126
Zierikzee, 99
Zuider Zee, 9, 94, 118
Zumthor, Paul, 140, 188

A Note About the Author

Anthony Bailey is the author of two novels and three nonfiction books. His most recent book was the much loved The Thousand Dollar Yacht; *and he has written of the environments men create for themselves in* Through the Great City *and* The Inside Passage. *Mr. Bailey's work has also appeared in* The New York Times, Horizon, *and* The New Yorker, *for which he is a staff writer.*

Mr. Bailey was born in England in 1933 and educated at Oxford. He now lives in Stonington, Connecticut, with his wife and four daughters.

A Note on the Type

This book was set on the Linotype in a face known as Modern No. 21. The "modern" part is a family name. It indicates that Number 21 is a great-great-grandchild of faces that were modern in 1800 — new as compared with the eighteenth-century types that preceded them, such as Caslon.

Composed, printed, and bound by
The Haddon Craftsmen, Inc.
Scranton, Pa.
Typography and binding design by
Virginia Tan